DOUGLAS COUNTY
CHRONICLES

DOUGLAS COUNTY
CHRONICLES

*HISTORY from the LAND
of ONE HUNDRED VALLEYS*

R.J. GUYER

THE
History
PRESS

Reedsport

Drain

Yoncalla

Oakland
Sutherlin

Winston

Roseburg

Myrtle Creek

Riddle

Canyonville

Glendale

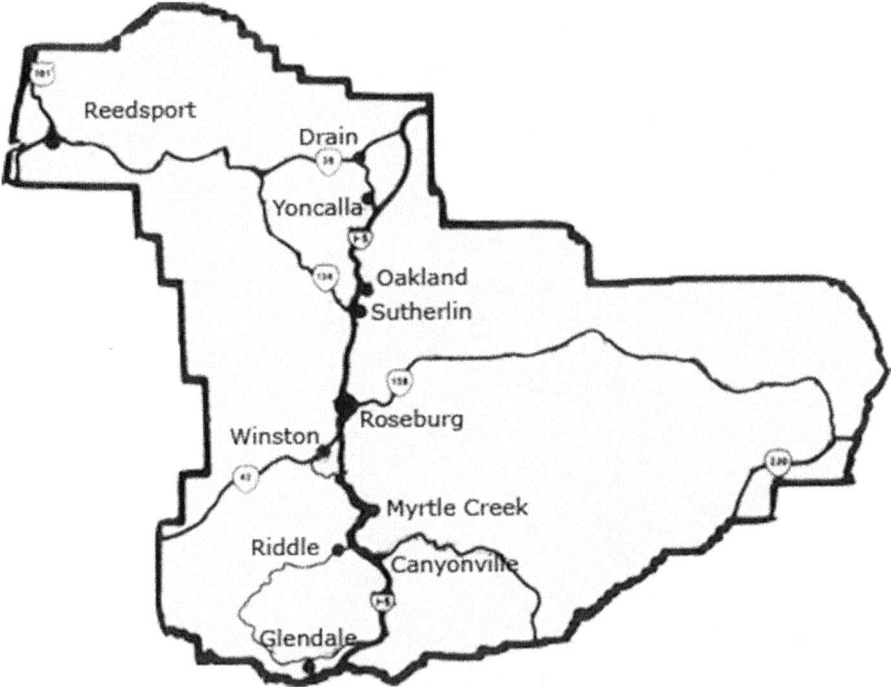

Map of Douglas County, Oregon. *Courtesy of the* News Review.

Published by The History Press
Charleston, SC 29403
www.historypress.net

Front cover: Original artwork depicting Douglas County by local artist Jan Barba Horn. Her work is displayed in galleries worldwide, including the White House.

Back cover, top: The Glendale Band. *Left*: Mildred Kanipe. *Both images courtesy of the Douglas County Museum.*

First published 2013

ISBN 978.1.5402.3230.4

Library of Congress CIP data applied for.

For my parents, Renwick and Julia Guyer, who instilled in me the values of family and community.

Contents

Foreword

C lick. Click. Click. In its 150 years of influence, photography has truly
changed the world. Photographic images literally capture moments in
time and provide us with the opportunity to tell their historic stories.

From its eastern boundary in the Cascades to its western edge along the
Pacific Ocean at the Oregon Dunes, Douglas County, also referred to as the
"Land of Umpqua," is unique in many ways. For thousands of years, this rich
region supported a multitude of Native American communities, including the
Cow Creek Band of the Umpqua tribe of Indians, many of whom still live in
the valley today. Amazing archaeological discoveries by the Bureau of Land
Management and the National Forest Service are documenting new periods
of previously unrecorded history. Some of these finds were preserved by the
explosion of Mount Mazama, which created today's Crater Lake.

Thousands of years later, this area became the southernmost post of the
Hudson's Bay Company, which in the 1820s hosted the botanical explorer
David Douglas. Douglas collected thousands of plant specimens throughout
the Northwest, including, in 1826, the sugar pine from just outside present-
day Roseburg and a tree that would become the center of a booming timber
industry, the Douglas fir. More explorations soon followed. Prospectors of
the California gold rush and pioneers from the Applegate Trail settling a new
frontier expanded the occupation of the valley. In the Victorian era, Douglas
County blossomed into the foundations of our communities today. It is in
this period that the first moments in time were captured by photograph in
Douglas County.

The era of innovation that brought photography to the Land of Umpqua was ushered in by the arrival of the railroad. The tracks that brought the Oregon & California Railroad to Roseburg were laid in 1872 and remained the end of the line until 1887. The railroad facilitated booms in the timber and agricultural industries, while also allowing for growth in tourism. People came from around the country to experience fly fishing in our rivers and hiking in our forests. The natural resources of Douglas County extended further than just the trees. Chinook, coho and steelhead were pulled from the waters of the Umpqua River, canned and exported. After the 1906 earthquake, much of San Francisco was rebuilt using timber from Douglas County.

Douglas County Chronicles is filled with a sampling of pictures captured over the first century of photography. We at the Douglas County Museum in Roseburg, Oregon, hold more than twenty-five thousand images of life in the Umpqua Valley and are excited to be a part of this storytelling process. Some of these images go all the way back to before Oregon was a state, to when Abraham Lincoln was president. These photos provide direct evidence of a very different world, both socially and environmentally. We are truly fortunate to have such a marvelous collection through which to glimpse this region's past. We are also grateful that this book has been created to share such wondrous visual stories with you. That is, after all, the true purpose of museums such as our own: to help inform the future by preserving glimpses of the past.

Gardner Chappell
Director, Douglas County Museum/Umpqua Lighthouse Museum
President, Oregon Museums Association

Acknowledgements

A special thanks to:

B.J. Bassett, my writing instructor and mentor, who encouraged me to step out of my comfort zone and be a writer. Thanks for your friendship.

My dear friend and fellow author of history Betty Kruse Smith. Without your guidance and encouragement, this book might never have gotten off the ground. Thanks also for checking the accuracy of the facts in this book.

Madalyn Tower for your coordination of all the e-mails and mailings in a timely manner and keeping the lines of communication open.

My wife, Ann Caldwell, for proofreading all the material and rewrites. Most of all, for your unyielding support throughout the duration of this project.

Craig Reed and Vicki Menard. It is a privilege to write for the *News Review*.

Gardner Chappell, Karen Bratton and Richard McQuillan of the Douglas County Museum for your support of facts and images for the book.

Esther Stutzman for sharing your extensive knowledge on the Native Americans and your friendship. Thank you for your dedication to the Indian Summer Camp, which provides a free weeklong camp for Indian children.

Sabra Unrath Wood for sharing your personal story with me. Yours was my most compelling interview for the book. I am deeply grateful for the opportunity to have met you and to share your emotional journey with others.

George and Lael Weigum for sharing your vast knowledge of Douglas County history.

John Robertson of the Douglas County Historical Society for sharing your insights and connections.

Jan Horn for your wonderful contribution of an original painting for the book.

The Pioneer Indian Museum in Canyonville. Marilyn Chandler, Lillian Stevenson and Ruth Ann Shuman for sharing your knowledge of South County history.

To Carmen Miles and the staff at the Douglas County Surveyor's Office.

To Aubrie Koenig, commissioning editor at The History Press, for your guidance throughout the writing of the book.

This project was a community effort and could not have been accomplished without help from James Marr, Gertie Eaton, Ed Eaton, Jana Whitaker, Alexis Burke, Syd Boyle, Miles Mitchell, Tony Tringolo, Romey Ware, Dave Rammage, Charles Lee, Erika Carlyle and John and Sue Hatfield.

Introduction

D ouglas County, Oregon, spans over five thousand square miles of varied terrain, west from the Pacific Ocean to the east, where its boundaries lie in the mountainous western Cascades. The land mass is larger in size than the state of Connecticut. A thumbprint of the county enters the northwestern tip of Crater Lake National Park, where centuries ago the twelve-thousand-foot volcano Mount Mazama blew its top and imploded, forming Crater Lake. The local native people called it the "Mountain with a Hole in the Top." It was considered sacred ground and was approached with reverence and awe.

Before the land was Douglas County, the Native Americans referred to it as the Land of the Umpqua. The land is dissected east to west by the cascading waters of the North and South Umpqua Rivers. From their origins high in the western Cascade Mountains, the rivers provided natives with both an abundant food source and a reliable mode of transportation to the region's western flank, the Pacific Ocean.

This book is not merely a manuscript depicting how Douglas County was formed. It is a collection of the stories of pioneers who migrated over rough, unknown terrain with a spirit of adventure to explore and settle the land. The book chronicles not only the successes but also the failures over the years. It is a celebration of that frontier spirit that has pervaded the region, demonstrating the resolve of its people to overcome tragedies along the way.

The journey begins with the first encounters between Europeans and Native Americans in 1791, when Captain James Baker reported anchoring a trading vessel, the *Jenny*, in Winchester Bay and successfully trading with the Lower Umpqua people. The Hudson's Bay Company then sent fur traders to the region and, in 1836, established a fort near Elkton. "Manifest Destiny" became the motto of the 1840s, bringing early settlers, including the famed Applegate Party, into the area.

The formation of Douglas County actually begins with a tale of two counties. Umpqua County was formed in 1851. At one time, it held portions of present-day Coos, Lane and Benton Counties. The Umpqua County seat became Elkton, while the bustling shipping port of Scottsburg was its business hub. Douglas County was formed in 1852 with a portion of Umpqua County up to Calapooya Creek, which served as the dividing line. Initially, the county seat was Winchester; however, in the election of 1854, the voters chose Deer Creek (present-day Roseburg) to become the county seat.

Umpqua County began to experience financial difficulties, which were exasperated by the flood of 1861. This led to a meeting between the "founding fathers" of both counties. It was decided that Umpqua County would be absorbed into what is now Douglas County.

1
Getting Here

Early History

A PLACE IN TIME

It is virtually impossible to know with exact certainty who were the first Europeans to set foot in Umpqua and Douglas Counties. After Cortes conquered Mexico in 1521, Spain was joined by England, Russia and France in a continued search of more treasures throughout the Pacific. Expeditions imperiously set out to chart and map the Pacific Northwest coastline. Scientists accompanied many voyagers during the height of the Enlightenment Movement of the eighteenth century. Soon, interest arose at the prospect of trapping in the Pacific Northwest, which held an abundance of fur for trading. Unfortunately, there is little known regarding any evidence of inland pursuits in this area of Oregon until after 1700.

Early maritime records indicate that in 1791, Captain James Baker, while sailing the English brig *Jenny*, entered the Umpqua Estuary. This voyage is considered to be the first non-Indian ship to cross the Umpqua Bar. According to the ship's log, it stayed approximately twelve days to trade with the Lower Umpqua Indians, who approached the ship in their dugout canoes. In 1792, Captain Charles Bishop sailed a trading vessel, the *Ruby* (the *Jenny*'s sister ship), into the Umpqua Harbor and also successfully traded with the Indians.

The United States continued its own version of "Enlightenment" on April 30, 1803, when President Thomas Jefferson agreed to the Louisiana

Purchase. The purchase extended the country's western borders into the Rocky Mountains and doubled the size of the United States. But Jefferson was not finished yet. Anxious to explore the new territory, he commissioned Meriwether Lewis and William Clark to "find the most direct and practical water communication across the continent." Along with mapping the territory for commercial opportunities, the group was equipped to study plant and animal species along the way.

The Lewis and Clark Expedition reached the convergence of the Columbia River and the Pacific Ocean on November 15, 1805. They spent the winter in a log building at Fort Clatsop, near today's Astoria, Oregon. Their discoveries led to a feverish expansion and competition of fur trappers and traders who settled along the river. To better compete, John Jacob Astor dissolved his American Fur Company in 1810, joining with new partners to form the Pacific Fur Company. In March 1811, they had established a post near the mouth of the Columbia River: Fort Astoria. However, two years later, the fort was rechristened Fort George by the Northwest Fur Company.

The ownership of Fort George was transferred once again in 1821, when the Northwest Fur Company merged with the Hudson's Bay Company. In an effort to expand its presence, George Simpson, the head of western operations for the Hudson's Bay Company, promoted Dr. John McLoughlin to chief factor for the Columbia District of the Oregon country. They began construction of Fort Vancouver at the confluence of the Willamette and Columbia Rivers in 1825. Author and historian Stephen Dow Beckham wrote, "Over the next twenty years Fort Vancouver became the hub of the fur trade in the region." But Simpson's vision was far more reaching, and he set his sights inland, to the south over the Calapooya Mountains, entering into the Umpqua watershed.

EARLY EXPLORERS

David Douglas

In 1823, Scottish botanist David Douglas sailed to New York. He had been commissioned by the Royal Horticultural Society of London to catalogue seeds and cuttings of trees to send back to England. He explored the eastern United States and into southeastern Canada. In Philadelphia, he studied plant samples from the Lewis and Clark Expedition. Douglas then applied for and received a sponsorship by the Hudson's Bay Company to inventory plant species along the Columbia River.

He arrived at Fort Vancouver on the boat *William and Ann* in April 1825 and lived in Fort Vancouver. While collecting samples in the Pacific Northwest, he was impressed by a large evergreen towering above that predominated the landscape. He referred to it as the "Oregon Pine" in his registry of samples. This unique species of tree would later be named for him: the Douglas fir.

It was Douglas's quest for another tree he had learned of—the sugar pine— that led him into the Umpqua Valley. He obtained permission to accompany Hudson's Bay Company explorer Alexander McLeod on his reconnaissance of the area in September 1826. McLeod had procured Umpqua Indian chief Centrenose to guide him down the Umpqua River to the Pacific Ocean. The chief's son would lead Douglas south in search of the pine. Upon canoeing down the Umpqua River, Douglas camped near Deer Creek and present-day Roseburg. He drew a sketch of the pine tree cone for an area Indian, who led him to a grove of "beautiful and immensely Grand Trees." The largest of the sugar pine trees measured almost 52 feet in circumference and stood about 245 feet tall. He also recorded data on other pines and plants in the area. Many of the specimens he collected are still in existence today in England. In addition to his botany records, the legacy of David Douglas also lives on through his diary. He gave some of the first European (non-Indian) accounts of the Douglas County area that he observed in 1826.

In July 1834, Douglas was working in Hawaii when he met an untimely death at the age of thirty-four. While exploring there, he fell into an underground pit built to catch wild cattle. He was gored by a large bull.

The world's tallest sugar pine tree stands in a grove of Sugar Pines east of Tiller. The grove is along Jackson Creek, a tributary of the South Umpqua River. It stands 265 feet tall with a diameter of almost eight feet. According to the National Forest Service, this is enough lumber to build five average houses. The sugar pine's cones are ten to twenty inches long.

The Hudson's Bay Company Fort Umpqua

In 1836, Hudson's Bay Company chief factor John McLoughlin's desire for a fur trading enterprise in the Umpqua Valley was finally realized. A site on the confluence of Elk Creek and the Umpqua River was chosen by John Baptiste Gagnier near present-day Elkton.

The site met the approval of McLoughlin's son-in-law, William Rae, and the small Fort Umpqua was built. It contained three buildings within a rectangular stockade 150 by 200 feet. There was a storehouse adjacent to the house for the trader in charge. Another building housed the employees. The fortified walls consisted of Douglas fir poles about 14 feet high, with only one gate entrance facing the river.

The fort employed about ten workers. Supplies and furs were hauled between Fort Vancouver and Fort Umpqua, over the Calapooia Mountains, using an established Indian trade route. The employees cleared and fenced eighty acres for farming and livestock operations. They introduced a variety of apples and vegetables to the region, in addition to creating a thriving fur trade with the Native Americans. In 1851, the fort was destroyed by fire. However, the Hudson's Bay Company maintained a post there until discontinuing operations in 1854.

Jedediah Strong Smith

After delivering supplies from Utah to California, Jedediah Smith and his men were told to leave California immediately. The governor in San Diego considered them to be trespassing. So the legendary mountain man headed north to Oregon with his party of eighteen men in July 1828. Known for his ability to lead expeditions through uncharted territory, Smith was living up to an earlier proclamation: "I wanted to be the first to view a country on which the eyes of a white man had never gazed and to follow the course of rivers that run through a new land."

Expedition member Harrison Rogers recorded that they crossed the Umpqua River and camped at its junction with what was later named the Smith River. The trappers were followed closely by the local Lower Umpqua (Kalawatset) Indians. According to Rogers, trouble began on July 12 when one of the natives was accused of stealing an axe.

On the morning of July 14, Smith put Rogers in charge and instructed him not to allow the Indians into camp due to the strained relationship. Richard Leland headed out with an Indian guide to explore the Smith River by canoe. Smith and John Turner left camp in search of a new trail for their party.

Meanwhile, Rogers ignored Smith's instructions and allowed the natives into the camp. Without warning, the Indians attacked the trappers in the camp, killing fourteen men. Arthur Black, although badly wounded, managed to escape. He fled up the coast and was escorted to Fort Vancouver by friendly natives. Smith, Turner and Leland also retreated to Fort Vancouver.

In September, Hudson's Bay Company's chief factor McLoughlin sent Alexander McLeod and Smith back to the area along with Umpqua chief Centrenose to recover Smith's property and restore peace. McLoughlin would later write that the attack was provoked by the trappers' inappropriate advances toward the Indian women. Shortly thereafter, Smith sold his recovered furs for $2,600 and left the area.

In 1830, as Smith mourned the death of his mother, he realized that during his years as a mountain man he had neglected his family. He bought a farm along with a town house near St. Louis and sold his stake in the Rocky Mountain Fur Company. As part of the terms of the sale, he agreed to secure supplies for the company's owners. In 1831, on what was to be his last trip into the wilderness, Smith was attacked by Comanche Indians on the Santa Fe Trail while searching for water. He died south of Ulysses, Kansas, on May 27, 1831, at the age of thirty-two.

Stephen A. Douglas

Stephen Arnold Douglas was a strong proponent of Oregon's statehood, and Douglas County was named in his honor. Douglas, however, is probably best known for his 1858 debates with Abraham Lincoln, which led to his victory over Lincoln for an Illinois Senate seat. These debates largely revolved around the hot topic of that day: slavery. Douglas was a Democrat who supported slavery, while Lincoln was a Republican who opposed it. Small in stature, Douglas was dubbed the "Little Giant" for his strong leadership and skillful debating. Lincoln would later publish a book on the debates, further demonstrating his position. His book garnered public acclaim that would propel his nomination for president in 1860. Lincoln won the quadrennial presidential election, which pit him against Douglas and two other candidates.

Douglas had also promoted the land grant system for the Illinois Central Railroad. Under his plan, dubbed the "checkerboard compromise," the government would allow the railroad companies to build rails over public lands. The land was divided into one-mile-square "checkerboard" parcels, to be divided every other parcel between the railroad and the federal government. Their belief was: as the tracks went, people and commerce were sure to follow. This would increase the land value, and the railroad companies would profit from the sale of the land and continue to expand rails throughout the country. The "land grant" model would lead to an accelerated expansion of the rails west. This resulted in a boom for the Douglas County economy when the trains reached Roseburgh (present-day Roseburg) in 1872.

2
The Land and Its People

NATIVE AMERICANS

The records of history from the eighteenth and nineteenth centuries were primarily written by men of European descent. Their accounts are essentially about the white male figures of the times and their accomplishments. Records of this span of history from the Native American perspective are somewhat limited. The ancestral history of the Indian Nations was dependent on oral interpretation of stories passed down between generations. Without a written record, the rapid decline of their population with the arrival of the white settlers caused a loss of the voice of several generations.

Records of their customs and traditions were limited, based largely on the observations and perceptions of white explorers and settlers in the area. Today, some descendants of the native tribes have become storytellers who recount traditional wisdom through stories handed down by elders and family. These recollections offer valuable insights into and preservation of Indian culture.

Douglas County was home to five distinct tribes (bands) of Native Americans. The fertile valleys along the Umpqua Rivers lined by lush forests provided a wide variety of nuts, plants and animals to sustain their diets.

The Kalawatset

The Kalawatset or Lower Umpqua Indians were first mentioned by early explorers in 1791. The natives approached the ships in their dugout canoes made of red cedar trees to trade salmon and otter skins for goods, including iron. They lived in rectangular cedar-planked homes in small villages along the Pacific and Lower Umpqua River estuary. In summer, they also lodged in traditional canvas tents.

Their area is home to the unique myrtle trees called *wegenhl* in their dialect. The myrtlewood nut, called *shichils*, provided an interesting food source. The raw nuts, which were bitter, were roasted and eaten whole, often with salmon eggs. The roasted nuts also made interesting flavors of coffee. The flavors ranged from burnt popcorn to a bitter chocolate taste.

Medicine men and women were common in the villages, as the Kalawatset beliefs were steeped in superstition. Many traditions and customs, like the rite of passage from childhood to adulthood, were immersed in gaining insights into the spirit world.

Today, the Lower Umpqua people are recognized as part of the Confederated Tribes of Coos, Lower Umpqua and Siuslaw Indians.

The Yoncalla

The Yoncalla tribe was a fragment of the Kalapuya (or Calapooia) tribe from the Willamette Valley that had become disenchanted with the fighting and dissension within the main tribe. Chief Halo led a group of approximately eighty members, known as the *Komemma*, south into the Yoncalla Valley. Eventually, the isolated Komemma created their own dialect by adding extra sounds or voice inflections to their native Kalapuyan language while also creating new words. In addition to abundant game for hunting, the valley offered a bounty of berries, plants and acorns, which they stored in the hollows of oak trees around the village of *Splachta alla*. The grass fields were burned in the fall to fertilize the soil and control insects. As a result of the burns, toasted grasshoppers were a treat for the tribe.

Today, Esther Stutzman is joined by daughters Shannin and Heather in a crusade to teach and continue the traditional ways of the Komemma people. They have shouldered the welfare of the Native American youth by establishing the Yoncalla Indian Education Program.

The Crossroads

There was a confluence of Indian trails that joined together near Elkton. Natives and settlers frequented these trails and the North Umpqua River for travel throughout the county. A historic campsite and burial grounds were unearthed near Kellogg and Elkton. Near this site, there is a Hinds walnut tree (which is not native to Oregon) on Yellow Creek that is over 250 years old. The location of the tree further supports the theory that the region was traveled by nomadic Indians as well as natives living in Umpqua and Douglas Counties. No one tribe seems to have laid claim to this communal portion of land.

Another perplexing piece of history involves an Indian chief from this region. There are several accounts from early settlers of a chief, believed to be the same person but mentioned by different names. In his 1834 journal, John Work explains he was camped between the Calapooia and Umpqua. He referred to the local chief as Satarna. Another person referred to the chief as Latana. Alexander McLeod identified a chief in the area as an Umpqua chief. David Douglas and John McLoughlin both described a Chief Centrenose.

The Umpqua People

The Umpqua people of the North Umpqua were considered shy and peaceful as they migrated between the seasons and salmon runs. They spent winters near present-day Winchester and camped from the Colliding Rivers (Glide) to Diamond Lake during the spring and summer. Salmon was a mainstay of their diet, which was supplemented with camas bulbs, berries, elk and deer.

David Douglas described a village in 1826 as having "two lodges and 25 people. The men wore shirts and trousers of undressed deerskins, some decorated with sea shells." Bridal customs of the Umpqua, like many native cultures, involved "bride prices" that were paid by the groom's family for marriage rights. The tribe entombed their dead in small plank houses and overturned canoes. There are mounds of stone piled at Susan Creek that are believed to be memorials to the dead. A small evacuation found no evidence of artifacts or burial sites.

Chief Nez-zac was their leader when the first settlers arrived in the 1840s. He died in February 1856, during the time the soldiers were rounding up Indians for the reservations. Much knowledge of the Umpqua people came from Chief Meshe (Mace) Tipton, who with his wife, Nance, lived into the twentieth century. Meshe was part of a band of Indians who escaped the soldiers and hid out along the Little River near Glide.

The Molalla

The Molalla people in Douglas County represented the southern range of the tribe, which extended as far north as the Molalla River in Clackamas County. This small band lived in the hills of the western Cascades primarily along the North and South Umpqua Rivers. A small amount of recorded history indicates they lived in underground houses during the winter. They also decorated their bodies with tattoos and cremated their dead. The Molalla was the last tribe in Douglas County to sign a treaty with Indian agent Joel Palmer, probably due to its small numbers and remote location.

The Molalla roots are linked to the mythological coyote known throughout Native American culture. According to Molalla folklore, Coyote was heading toward Mount Hood when he met Grizzly Bear. Grizzly Bear asked, "Where are you going, Coyote?"

Coyote said, "I am going upcountry."

"Why are you going up there?" inquired Grizzly Bear.

Coyote answered, "I am making the world."

Then Grizzly Bear said, "We must fight."

The story tells how cunning Coyote would challenge Grizzly Bear instead to a duel. They would swallow hot stones for supremacy. Coyote tricked Grizzly Bear by swallowing five strawberries. Grizzly Bear then swallowed the red-hot stones, which burst his heart. He was scattered across the area. This story signifies to the Molalla that they would always be strong hunters.

Kathryn Harrison, the Molalla's first female tribal leader, served as an advocate for her people, helping the tribe gain federal recognition in 1983. Harrison followed in the footsteps of her great-aunt "Molalla Kate," who worked with young girls to pass along the crafts of making baskets and stringing bead necklaces.

The Cow Creek Band

The Cow Creek Band of the Umpqua continues to make its home in the southern county. For centuries, its homeland has been the fertile valleys that lie between the Coastal Range and the western foothills of the Cascade Mountains. Myrtle Creek is situated in the northern aspect of its land, which once abutted the lands of the southern Molalla tribe.

Unlike other tribes where a single leader spoke for the entire people, each village of the Cow Creek Band was somewhat independent, having its own chief. However, Chief Miwaleta was recognized by most as the band's leader. As pioneer settler George Riddle pointed out in his book *Early Days in Oregon*, "The Indians seemed to regard him with reverence more than fear."

Similar to the other Umpqua peoples, hunting and fishing provided the mainstay of their diet, along with nuts, berries and camas bulbs. Huckleberries were a favorite of the Cow Creek. Around mid- to late August, they would camp for weeks near the huckleberry patches in the mountains along their southern region known as the Rogue-Umpqua Divide. The Rogue River tribes of the Latgana and Takelma joined in the picking, which was also a social time of telling stories and catching up in the Takelma dialect. The berry picking was followed closely by the salmon runs in the area's rivers and streams. The Cow Creek had a unique way of catching salmon. They used funnel-shaped baskets made of hazel shoots that were strung across the stream to catch the fish.

Over time, tensions began to build between the southern Indians and the white settlers. In 1834, Ewing Young's party of trappers murdered several Native Americans and buried their bodies. Their bodies were later discovered near their trapping camp. When miners entered the area along the Applegate Trail, they showed little regard for the Indian way of life or their homeland. The hydraulic mining destroyed much of the salmon habitat. Overhunting in the area made food scarce. Meanwhile, entire forests of maple and oak trees were cut down.

Chief Miwaleta was an advocate of peace, and he hoped that by signing a federal treaty with the government in 1853 he could save the way of life and the future of the Cow Creek Nation. This was the first federal treaty signed by a tribe in the Pacific Northwest.

The government took advantage of the Indians by agreeing to pay 2.3 cents per acre for land that was being sold to settlers for $1.25 an acre. There was also a promise to give the Cow Creek Indians a sixty-thousand-acre reservation. However, Miwaleta died soon afterward, and when some of the men from the tribe joined in the Rogue Indian Wars of 1855–56, the United States claimed the aggressions broke the treaty. The Cow Creek Band never received the land it was promised. The Bureau of Indian Affairs began transitioning Indians north to the Siletz and Grand Ronde reservations. Local militias hunted down remaining members, looking to rid the area of all tribal members. Seven families survived by hiding out in the upper Umpqua region.

Sue Shaffer

Beginning in 1979, legislation was signed by President Carter and, later, Ronald Reagan that allowed tribes to file suit with the U.S. Court of Claims for restitution for lands that were taken away from them. Members of the seven surviving families filed in accordance with the legislation. However, Congress, along with the Bureau of Indian Affairs, ruled that the seven members had not proven their heritage. Tribal chairwoman Sue Shaffer of Canyonville took on the fight for the families, and finally, in 1984, Congress agreed to settle with the tribe for the lost revenue they had been promised over 130 years before. Instead of divvying up the money separately to individuals, the resourceful Shaffer put the money away, and the interest has been allocated for tribal needs, including infrastructure improvements and healthcare.

Under the direction of Sue Shaffer, a 450-seat bingo hall was expanded several times to become Oregon's first full-scale Indian casino. Currently, there is a 298-room hotel and a large RV park to accommodate over one million visitors annually. The Cow Creek tribe manages several other businesses along with the casino, in addition to overseeing four thousand acres of property. The Cow Creek tribe is alive and well. It is demonstrating Sue Shaffer's motto: "We build people here, not dependency."

Legacy

The once-proud Native American tribes in Douglas County were decimated by diseases of the white settlers. Although they were peaceful, the uprisings of Indians in the Rogue River area caused fear in the white settlers. Indian agent Joel Palmer's report stated, "The Indians were to be divorced of their native lifestyles and forced to adopt the ways of 'civilization.'" This was to be carried out in the "utmost good faith."

Many natives moved willingly after several treaties were ratified. Others were rounded up by soldiers and led to the Grand Ronde or Siletz reservations on what was called the "Trail of Tears." Today, strides have been made to bury past indiscretions, which has led to mutual respect and understanding of the different cultures.

SETTLERS ARRIVE

The 1840s saw a large migration of people heading westward along the Oregon Trail, while others arrived via ships that steamed around South America via Cape Horn to reach Oregon. Emigrants were guided by the alluring promises of the unsettled wide-open spaces and inexpensive land claims. Many settlers sought to make a new start in this untamed territory. Western expansion was sparked further in 1845, when John O' Sullivan, editor of the *New York Morning Post*, expressed, "It is our manifest destiny... to possess the whole of the continent which Providence has given for us the development of the great experiment of liberty." The decade would end with another rush of prospectors in search of gold. The terminus of the Oregon Trail for most was Oregon City. From this point, settlers quickly dispersed in all directions to stake their land claims.

The Applegate Trail

Jesse Applegate and his wife, Cynthia Ann (Parker), owned a large farm in St. Clair County, Missouri. When the surrounding farms began to replace hired hands with slaves, Jesse, who was vehemently opposed to slavery, decided to leave Missouri for Oregon. In April, his brothers, Charles and Lindsay, and their families joined him on the two-thousand-mile Oregon Trail during the "Great Migration of 1843." Many travelers walked the entire route, barefoot. According to statistics, approximately one in ten died along the route over the years. Cholera and accidents involving wagons were the main culprits.

The Applegates arrived at Fort Walla Walla, Washington, in November. Here, the decision was made to leave behind their wagons and cattle for a quicker trip on small boats down the Columbia River to reach the Willamette Valley. Near The Dalles, Oregon, Jesse and Lindsay watched in horror as a boat that carried their sons overturned in the rapids. Both of their sons, along with boat guide Alexander McClellan, drowned. The Applegates and others in their party pledged to find a safer route into the Willamette Valley by avoiding the river entirely.

Lindsay and Jesse traveled west into the Willamette Valley and settled in what is now Polk County, Oregon. In 1846, a party of fifteen men departed to blaze the North and South Trail. Jesse, a former surveyor, was captain, with Lindsay riding as second in command. Each man headed out with a saddled horse, a packhorse and supplies. The group headed south following the established trails of the Hudson's Bay Company explorers and trappers.

The men entered the Yoncalla Valley mid-morning on June 25. In her book *The Halo Trail*, Anne Applegate Kruse describes the scene: "Meadows grass, waist high, undulated in the breeze. One member of the party named it horse heaven." Anxious to move on, they resolved to return and settle in the area. Unbeknownst to them, the group was under close observation by Chief Halo and his people.

The party followed the route to its end at Bear Creek Valley in southern Oregon. From here, they blazed a new trail they dubbed the "Southern Road," heading eastward toward the Lower Klamath Lake. The trail then took a more southerly direction, crossing the Black Rock Desert to reach the Humboldt River. Here it connected with the California Trail. The Applegate Trail proved to be a safe and viable alternative route for pioneers. It also became a popular route south during the gold rush in California.

The Halo Trail

The Halo Trail is an ancient Indian trail that meanders from the Calapooia Mountains through the Yoncalla Valley. The trail passed the village of *Splachta alla* (meaning "birds of the valley"), where Chief Halo and his people lived. *Splachta alla* was the last remaining traditional Indian village in the region. Chief Halo and his people were a fragment of the Calapooia tribe. The name *Halo* is Chinook, meaning "having nothing or poor in worldly goods."

Halo's great-great-granddaughter Esther Stutzman, who is an expert in the history of the Kalapuya people, explains that Chief Halo's given name was *Camafeena*, which translates to "ferns that grow from the ground." She also points out that the proper name given to this local Indian tribe is *Komemma*, and they are part of the Kalapuya Nation.

After establishing the famed trail, the Applegate Party returned to stake land claims in the area governed by Chief Halo. Instinctually, one might

Chief Halo (*Camafeena*), photo from the 1860s. Halo was chief of the *Komemma* people. *Photo courtesy of the Douglas County Museum.*

envision a battle of bow and arrow and guns near the traditional Indian village of *Splachta alla*. Although history may have given both sides reason to be somewhat apprehensive, both parties demonstrated respect toward the other. There was constructive dialogue spoken in the Chinook language as they exchanged gifts. This laid the foundation for a peaceful coexistence. Halo was impressed with the craftsmanship of the Applegate houses, so they built him a cabin and garden area in which to live. Halo enjoyed gardening but always wondered why the white women planted flowers in their gardens when there was an abundance of beautiful flowers growing naturally.

In her book, Anne Applegate Kruse gives a detailed account of the valley's history through many stories of the trials, tribulations and even celebrations of the times. The great sense of community spirit comes alive at one of their festive celebrations on the Fourth of July: "The morning of the fourth dawned clear and beautiful…in an old oak grove along Elk Creek on Uncle Albert Applegate's farm. The Indians were there, people came from miles around. It was a gay and festive scene. The men set up long tables. Great baskets and boxes of food were brought in from buggy, hack or even farm wagon." There was roasted and fried chicken with dressing and "seven kinds of cakes and pies galore."

One day, a government agent came to the valley and insisted that Chief Halo move to a nearby reservation. The chief stood defiant, "Shoot. I am no coward. I will die here and be buried among my people." The Applegate brothers stepped in and took responsibility. "He lived, died [1878] and is buried, as was his wish, in *Splachta alla*. In the last autumn of his life he continued coming around the hill to visit his beloved white brother, Charles Applegate."

A LASTING FRIENDSHIP

History doesn't repeat itself—at best it sometimes rhymes.
—Mark Twain

In 1973, a subdivision was proposed in the heart of the land Chief Halo refused to leave. Susan and Shannon Applegate stood up with others to successfully oppose the development. It threatened not only the hallowed Indian burial ground but also the sacred Indian "Halo" Rock. This large rock has deeply cut markings and drawings. Many attempts have been made by outsiders to translate the meaning of these petroglyphs. "There are some things that don't need to be revealed. Our people know what it says to us and it is sacred," Esther Stutzman explains. "The area is now on private property."

Anne Applegate Kruse offers the following translation in her book *The Halo Trail*:

> *Dim the valley slumbers underneath the waning moon, the chilly breath of autumn chants in shifting, vibrant rune. 'Mong the unmarked graves of ancients whose age long need of fame was written on the sacred rock before*

Sumner Brawn standing by the sacred Halo Rock. The petroglyph carvings were made by the Yoncalla Indians, a part of the Calapooia tribe of the Umpqua. The message is believed to be a record of a battle with another tribe. *Photo courtesy of the Douglas County Museum.*

the white man came. We mark the trail in Halo's name, record the ancient lore, but they who trod the winding path will walk it nevermore.

Today, Stutzman works diligently to preserve the history of the Kalapuya Indians as a storyteller. Her projects include the Yoncalla Indian Education Program, and for the past thirty-six years she has run a weeklong Indian Summer Camp that takes place in July for grades four through twelve.

Near Yoncalla, the house built in 1852 by Charles and Melinda Applegate remains in the Applegate family. This structure houses the nonprofit Heritage Arts and Education Organization that offers programs and events that focus awareness on the traditional arts and ways of the Kalapuya Indians and early American settlers. The site director is author Shannon Applegate, the workshop coordinator is artist Susan Applegate and the chair of the board is Esther Stutzman. The three are descendants of Chief Halo and the Applegate families. History has come full circle as the three not only work together but also sing in a group called The Slow Ponies that entertains locally. Together, they are preserving a friendship that has been sustained for over 160 years.

The Umpqua Land Company

An intriguing mix of chance meetings led to the formation of the Umpqua Land Company. Job Hatfield had been a bar pilot, guiding vessels across the hazardous waters of the Columbia River Bar. In 1850, he led a group of men south to explore the Umpqua River Bar. While there, they met Jesse Applegate and Levi Scott, who were surveying present-day Scottsburg.

At the same time, the ship *Samuel Roberts* entered the Umpqua River with members of California's "Klamath Exploring Expedition" who had chartered the vessel to explore the Umpqua River. Their mission was to acquire land at strategic points for the establishment of town sites along the river and near existing trails to mines.

When the Applegate and Hatfield parties learned of the expedition's intentions as land speculators, they met to form a joint venture. The group founded the Umpqua Land Company in August 1850. Most of the investors were successful businessmen who agreed that all land claims by the company would be divided equally into shares. Members of the party included, among others, Jesse Applegate, Job Hatfield, Herman Winchester and Horace Paine. Some of these partners would become the founding fathers of Umpqua and Douglas Counties.

The company, however, was disbanded later that fall when the territory legislature passed the Donation Land Act, which prohibited companies and nonresidents from holding land for speculation. The group did establish future sites for several towns, including Winchester and Umpqua City.

Surveying the County

Looking back on the days of homesteading and land claims in Douglas County, it is easy to overlook a critical step in the entire process. The land had to be fairly divvied up between the settlers in accordance with their land claims. This led to the creation of an important political position in county government: the county surveyor. Rancher George W. Jones was elected as Douglas County's first surveyor in 1860.

The Donation Land Claim Act of 1850 was passed by Congress to promote settlement in the Oregon Territory. The act allowed every unmarried male, eighteen years of age or older, 320 acres and every

George W. Jones, the first county surveyor, was elected to office in 1860. He was an accomplished musician and loved to play the fiddle at events. *Photo courtesy of Romey Ware.*

married couple 640 acres. It was necessary for land claims to be surveyed to acquire title, which was dependent on first establishing the rectangular system of townships and sections. This was needed to create control for surveying the claims. Townships were created in six- by six-mile parcels or thirty-six-square-mile increments.

In theory, it seems like quite an easy task—just measure the squares and place the markers. However, Douglas County is populated with forests that span rugged mountainous terrain. In 1860, George measured the sections with the use of a staff compass and a sixty-six-foot-long chain called a Gunter's Chain. (The chain was created in 1620 by English mathematician Edmund Gunter.) The painstaking, labor-intensive process required creating a true line with the compass and measuring with the chain. The sections were eighty lengths of chain long by eighty wide. Trees, streams and hills had to be allotted for when making calculations. The plat distances were measured

35

horizontally, so on hills the chain would be broken as needed to compensate for the angles to get an accurate horizontal measurement. Trigonometry was used for the angles and done by hand in the field.

Surveyor Romey Ware explains, "The courts ruled early on that the original surveyed positions held, unless there was gross negligence. Some sections may only measure 79.4 chains instead of the full 80. The original marker remains the property's marker." Romey Ware followed in his great-grandfather George Jones's footsteps when he became the Douglas County surveyor in 1997. In 2004, he received the prestigious Oregon Surveyor of the Year Award. "About all that had changed from the time George [Jones] was surveyor was the equipment became more sophisticated," Romey recounts.

3
Transportation

OVER THE RIVER

Ferries

Early on, most of the routes that led through the county had at least one stream or river to cross. Initially, funds were not available to warrant the building of bridges, so entrepreneurs began offering ferry services for safer crossing. Most ferry owners enjoyed a monopoly, as it was usually neither feasible nor economical to have more than one ferry per river crossing. To implement fair practices and standards for ferries, the Oregon Territory legislature passed "An Act Regulating Ferries" in 1849. The legislation put county courts in charge of establishing rates and taxes on the ferries. With the power to grant business licenses, there was also mention of not abusing that power to show favoritism. Another requirement of the law regarding the safety of passengers was that a ferryman must provide "a good tight boat."

Many of the crafts were flat-bottomed scows about twelve feet wide and forty feet long. There were a variety of ways to cross the streams. Most ferrymen guided the craft over the current with an overhead cable; still others used winches. A few ferries were pulled by mules.

Even with the establishment of regulations for ferry travel, there were conflicts that arose. In 1905, an incident occurred on the Lone Rock Ferry

The Lone Rock Ferry carrying a covered wagon, circa 1900. The ferry, located by the community of Glide, was founded by Warren Hughes. *Photo courtesy of the Douglas County Museum.*

at Glide. Warren Hughes established the ferry service in 1878, initially using a pole to guide the craft over the river before switching to a cable. The ferry was later sold to Douglas County, which operated it as a free ferry.

Leona Mathews accepted a teaching job at Lone Rock School. She set up to board with the Connie family and planned to walk to school. The trip from the Connie house to the school required crossing the river. However, the ferryman refused to use the ferry for just one passenger, so Mathews walked along the rocky shore and took an oar boat across the river. When Mr. Connie caught word of this, he immediately brought the matter up to the county judge in Roseburg. The judge ruled that the ferry was the property of Douglas County, and the ferryman was required to provide Mathews a ride across.

The Trenton Ferry, established near Elkton in 1851, involved a dispute over who had the rights to run the ferry. There was a lawsuit filed in the state Supreme Court in 1851 between Levi Grant and E.P. Drew over the matter. At times, the two had gone as far as each running ferries concurrently at the site. The suit and settlement were complicated, to say the least. Nine years later, when Grant sold out his claim to William Mills in 1860, Drew still claimed he owned the license to the ferry. Ironically, the large flood of 1861 wiped out most dwellings in the area. It would later become a free ferry operated by Douglas County.

Arguably one of the most profitable ferries was the Winchester Ferry that crossed the North Umpqua River on the Applegate Trail. One of the ferry owners, John Aiken, used his wealth to finance a portion of the Douglas National Bank.

The "Covered" Bridges of Douglas County

With scores of emigrants migrating and settling throughout Oregon, it was necessary to build bridges over the area's rivers and streams for safer and more permanent crossings. By the early 1900s, Oregon was estimated to have over four hundred covered bridges. It's hard to imagine that these landmarks of such aesthetic beauty were in fact built with a utilitarian purpose in mind. Frontiersmen utilized the plentiful Douglas firs in the area to build the bridges. The backbone of these historic bridges is the structural design of their foundation, with the use of sturdy wooden trusses. To protect the bridges from the elements, designs were borrowed from the eastern states, adding the rudimentary barn-like coverings. The covered bridges owe their longevity to this hardy craftsmanship.

There were a couple of rather large covered bridges crossing the North Umpqua River that are no longer in existence. In Glide, the Lone Rock Covered Bridge was built in 1922 by Elmer Metzer to replace a river ferry. This rare three-span bridge covered an incredible length of 315 feet. It was dismantled in 1959. The Winchester Bridge was built in 1859 by the Moore brothers. But it was destroyed in a statewide flood only two years later, in 1861. An eyewitness account noted, "The flood rose overnight to the floor of the [bridge], and then to the roof. The roof parted from the main structure, and went floating down stream, followed very shortly by the remainder of the bridge."

The Pass Creek Bridge in Drain, according to the Umpqua Historic Preservation Society, was built in 1906 to replace an original bridge on the site that was constructed on the Overland Stage Route in 1870. The popular stage route linked Jacksonville, Oregon, with the Willamette Valley. A horse-drawn wagon loaded with supplies for a Thanksgiving Turkey Shoot crashed

Mill Creek covered bridge on Highway 38 over Mill Creek, at the junction with the Umpqua River. *Photo courtesy of the Douglas County Museum.*

through the floor about 1920. The driver survived unscathed; however, several turkeys drowned, and supplies were lost in the river. In 1987, the bridge, including the Howe trusses, was dismantled, moved a block away and reassembled. Today, it can be seen behind the Drain Civic Center.

The Rochester Bridge is located northwest of Sutherlin. The bridge, which spans Calapooia Creek, features elegant curved-topped windows. The bridge was built by Floyd Frear in 1933. By the late 1950s, the bridge had begun to deteriorate. Fearing that the county might burn down the bridge and replace it, locals are said to have protected it with armed guards until the county renovated it in 1969. It was constructed with Howe trusses. The Neal Lane Bridge crosses over the South Myrtle Creek. It is distinguished as being the only King Post truss–designed bridge in Oregon. At only forty-two feet long, it is also among the shortest covered bridges in Oregon. The bridge is southeast of Myrtle Creek and is said to have been built in 1929 (however, some maintain that it was built in 1939).

The Horse Creek Bridge now stands in Myrtle Creek's Mill Site Park. Built in 1930, it originally spanned Horse Creek in Lane County. The bridge, built with Howe trusses, now spans the stream of Myrtle Creek.

The Milo Academy Bridge east of Canyonville spans the South Umpqua River and is known as Oregon's only steel girder bridge that is a covered wood bridge. As the story goes, the bridge was built in 1962 to replace a covered bridge from 1920. The residents of Milo missed the character of the original covered bridge, so the bridge was made to resemble the original. The bridge is privately owned.

Arguably, the most photographed bridge in Douglas County is the Cavitt Creek Bridge. Built in 1943 by Floyd Frear, the bridge stands about eight miles south of Glide near the site of the original Peel Store. The Howe Truss Bridge features Tudor arch portals. It is said the design was made to accommodate the many logging trucks in the area.

Many covered bridge owners charged a toll to help defray the building and maintenance costs. In fact, the Oregon Provisional Government's legislature passed an act in December 1845 concerning the matter of bridges. The act also established minimum toll fees. Architect Lee H. Nelson provides "an interesting index to frontier values established as 'Laws of a General and Local Nature, Passed by the Legislative Committee and Legislative Assembly'":

For every wagon and a single yoke or span of horses, mules	25 cents
A single horse and carriage	18 cents
A single footman	5 cents
A man and horse	10 cents
All other horses and cattle, per head	3 cents

Originally built to ensure the safer crossings of rivers and streams, the bridges of Douglas County offer a nostalgic trip back in time. Each picturesque bridge maintains its own character, influenced by its unique designs. These treasures remain as a viable slice of Americana.

THROUGH THE WOODS

Fancy yourself a traveler of the 1870s in Douglas County. Your imagination runs wild with thoughts of a romantic ride aboard a Concord stagecoach. A gentle breeze whispers as you indulge yourself with visions of carefree days on the open trail. The sun is high above in the cobalt-blue sky as the road meanders past rocky outcroppings lined by emerald green forests of firs and pines. At last, you take in the breathtaking panorama of the ocean waves crashing onto the golden sandy beaches.

While this may have been the case for some, most riders found the coaches to be a bit cramped and stuffy. Traveling during the rainy season often called for some passengers to get out and walk up hills. Others might be asked to help clear the stage axles and wheels of mud or even help to push the stage out of the deep ruts. The stages did, however, offer a viable alternative to riding horseback, and many stops along the routes offered good food and conversation. There were many stages in Douglas County. The following are a few of the more notable stage lines.

The Oregon–California Stage Company

This long-distance stage company was contracted for the daily delivery of mail between Portland and Sacramento in 1860. Up to this point, mail delivery used many different carriers and was unreliable. This company also delivered for the Wells Fargo Company. Mailbags were kept in the back of the coach while the drivers kept the money box up front near them.

The company owned twenty-eight coaches that were painted bright yellow with green trim, and it maintained about six thousand horses for use throughout the route. It employed thirty-five drivers. During good weather, it took about seven days each way. The first stage left Portland in September 1860. The company continued until the Oregon and California Railroad was awarded the contract to carry the mail. In Roseburg, a band played and the crowd cheered as driver Tom Burnett placed the last mail from Postmaster Harry Stanton into his stagecoach in August 1882.

The Coos Bay Wagon Road

Arguably one of the most scenic routes through Douglas County is the remote Coos Bay Wagon Road, which still follows along much of the original stage route today. Land for the road was originally given to the Oregon and California Railroad Company in 1866 under the land grant system. The government financed the project to be built and used as a military passage between the cities of Roseburg and Coos Bay.

Approximately seventy-four thousand acres of federal land had been retained in Coos and Douglas Counties for this purpose. However, the

Oregon and California Railroad Company was forced to forfeit the grant for failing to comply with its provisions. This led to the formation of the Coos Bay Wagon Road Company. The inaugural meeting for the stockholders of this new venture was held on March 22, 1869.

By 1872, wagons had begun to haul cargo and military equipment along the Wagon Road. With the arrival of the Concord stagecoach, the road was opened to passenger travel as well. In his book *Roughing It*, Mark Twain described the Concord coach as "a cradle on wheels."

Despite its spring suspension and other amenities such as leather seats and adjustable curtains, the coaches offered little protection against the many elements of the trail. The narrow bumpy road and curves posed hazards for the wagon axles and wheels. Wind-driven dust, rain and even snow found its way into the tiny coach, which measured about four feet wide and less than five feet high inside. With the curtains completely drawn, the cabin became dark and stuffy.

The fare was five dollars for the three-day trip. It was common to have up to six passengers per stage. A typical one-way trip used the services of five drivers and forty-two horses. Reston was the first stop for passengers starting from either Tenmile or Lookingglass. In Reston, the Arthur Johnson Place was built to accommodate stage travelers. The two-story house with two covered porches still stands today. The Weekly family ran a popular tavern in the town as well. From Reston, the sharp curving road continued steeply up Reston Ridge, providing a challenging trip for both passenger and horse.

The road then leveled out into the beautiful Brewster Canyon, named after early explorer Horace Brewster. Today, the pavement gives way to a narrowing gravel road for the next eleven miles. Rocky cliffs hug the north side of the road as the south side falls off rather steeply. The thick, deep forest engulfs the road under a picturesque canopy of trees.

In spite of this area's arresting beauty, the narrow roadway was a harrowing experience for the stage and wagon drivers. In places, there was no margin of error as the tight road offered little room on either side. It was important that the drivers maintained control of the horses while keeping the wheels from scraping the cliff walls or slipping over the edge on the opposite side.

Here, the valley's incline transforms the east fork of the Coquille River from a peaceful stream into a cascading river. Further along this stretch, there are many places to stop and revel in the solitude and admire the beauty of the area's many waterfalls.

Driving westward, the stage crossed over the county line into the town of Sitkum, which is a Chinook term meaning "half." Here, the Laird family ran the highly popular Halfway House. What began as a cabin expanded into a ten-bedroom lodge complete with a tavern, telegraph station and post office. Hungry travelers delighted in the delicious cooking of Nancy "Belle" Laird, remembered especially for her chicken and light bread biscuits. Belle, who ran the post office until she was eighty-three years old, is known fondly by locals as the "Mother of Brewster Valley." The Laird men were stage and wagon drivers. The Halfway House burned down in 1903, after which the Lairds later ran an auto stage line over the route. The road continues through the towns of Dora, McKinley and Fairview in Coos County before reaching the Eastside Neighborhood in Coos Bay.

The Drain—Coos Bay Stage Line

Similar to the beginning of the Coos Bay Wagon Road, the first attempt to establish a route between Drain and Coos Bay was made by a railroad company. The costly project set back the Southern Pacific Railroad Company over $1 million before it was discontinued. The trip from Drain to Coos Bay via stage was a one-of-a-kind adventure. In 1876, the wagon road was completed between Drain and Scottsburg. Leaving Drain, the Concord stages traveled along the Elk Creek and over Hancock Mountain into Elkton. Passengers enjoyed dining at Weatherly's Eating House. Here, the stage made a stop and would switch drivers and possibly horses from the Elkton horse barn.

During the rainy season, muddy roads impeded the progress of the stages, as mud would build up on the wheels and axles. Passengers were often asked to help in removing the sticky mess. When horses arrived covered in mud, they were immediately taken down to the river and washed off before it dried. A new team of horses would then lead the way to Scottsburg.

Harry Worthylake gave his account of riding this stage line:

My acquaintance with Oregon roads began at four o'clock in the morning of February 27, 1907, when my father and I boarded the stage at Drain and headed down (along) the Umpqua River to Scottsburg, the end of the road. There seemed to be three classes of passengers on, or rather with, the stage. First class passengers (women and babies) rode. Second class passengers (older men and small boys like me) walked up

The beach stage from Winchester Bay to Coos Bay, the final section of the Drain–Coos Bay stage line. This view shows two four-horse teams and one freight wagon. *Photo courtesy of the Douglas County Museum.*

all the hills. Third class passengers (able-bodied men like my father) walked up the hills and carried poles to pry the stagecoach out of the deeper mud holes. A change of horses at Elkton made it possible to get to Scottsburg the same day. The next day we rode the mail boat down river to Gardiner.

From Elkton, the road paralleled the Umpqua River to reach Scottsburg. Passengers wishing to complete the trip to Coos Bay lodged in Scottsburg and took a paddle-wheeled steamboat to Winchester Bay the next day. The *Restless*, which was built in Gardiner, carried both passengers and freight. Later, the popular steamboat *Eva* made daily trips on the route until 1916. Along with its passengers and freight, this boat also carried mail. Upon disembarking the boat in Winchester Bay, passengers rode a horse-drawn beach stage, which traveled over the sandy beaches during low tide, completing the trip to Coos Bay. The beach coaches were equipped with wider wheels to accommodate the softer sand.

MAKING TRACKS

Locomotion in Douglas County

On May 10, 1869, Leland Stanford drove in the golden spike at Promontory Summit, Utah, connecting the eastern and western United States with a transcontinental railroad. The project was the culmination of efforts by Congress, which in 1853 approved the War Department to conduct a survey for the rail. The next hurdle would be the funding for the project, which came as loan guarantees for each mile of track. The Congress also passed the Pacific Railway Act in 1862, using the checkerboard land grant system designed by Illinois senator Stephen Douglas, to encourage expansion of the railroads by dividing federal lands into one-mile-square sections. The railroad companies would receive every other section, which they could sell to fund continued building.

Even before the monumental golden spike was placed, plans were in action for a north-and-south railroad connecting Portland, Oregon, with Marysville, California. With a similar land grant system in place, the railroad companies forged ahead with the project in 1866. Gandy dancers (a slang term describing workers who laid track and maintained the lines) worked arduously to advance the tracks. What a sight it was on a crisp fall day in 1872; as the band played, residents of Roseburg lined the streets in anticipation of the arrival of its first locomotive. The excitement built to a fever pitch until finally, out came a collective sigh when the whistle blew. To the pleasure of the crowd, as steam rolled from the wood-burning engine, brakemen brought the powerful locomotive to a screeching halt.

The southern portion of the line had linked Marysville with Redding, California, in 1872, before work came to a halt. Financial difficulties plagued the railroad companies and European investors as well. For the next fifteen years, Roseburg would be the final stop on the southern run from Portland.

As the terminus of the line, the Roseburg population and economy boomed. The area around the depot was teeming with activity. A roundhouse and warehouses were built as supplies were loaded and unloaded. Early on, sheep and cattle were hot commodities and the bulk of the railroad's freight. At the south end of the rail yard, a stock pit was built to corral the animals for shipping. After World War II, as the timber industry expanded in Douglas County, lumber dominated the bills of freight. According to Roseburg attorney

Engine #1518 from the 1890s. Photo taken near the Roundhouse in Roseburg. *Photo courtesy of the Douglas County Museum.*

and railroad buff Charles Lee, "The railroad brought with it many jobs... track walkers were responsible for a mile section of the track, checking for problems such as loose spikes or deteriorating ties. Roseburg was a division point for train crews who covered 100 miles of track."

Several businesses near the depot served the railroad and its passengers. The Roseburg Hotel, on the corner of Lane and Sheridan Streets, lodged guests arriving via the train. A popular restaurant was the Harris Café, which was known for its homemade bread. Owner Lucie Harris was well respected by the rail workers because she made her place available for meals regardless of what time the trains rolled in.

The town of Sutherlin established a connecting rail to bring goods to the main line. The Weyerhaeuser Engine #100, displayed today in Sutherlin, was used to haul logs from a stand of timber known as the "Roach Unit," owned by the Roach Timber Company out of Iowa.

With the completion of Tunnel 13 high in the Siskiyou Mountains, the golden spike was hammered in just south of Ashland in 1887, thus completing the remaining route between California and Oregon. This opened up the rail to the southern Douglas County communities, with scheduled stops at depots in Myrtle Creek and Glendale.

The 4 percent grades and sharp curves in the Siskiyou Mountains would lead the Southern Pacific Railroad to open an alternative route in 1927, diverting much of the rail traffic from Springfield, Oregon, to Black Butte, California. Charles Lee explains, "The railroad was big in Roseburg (and surrounding areas) for years until they opened the [Natron] cutoff through Klamath Falls. The cutoff provided a shorter route with easier grades."

The railroad remains a proud tradition in Douglas County, although many changes have occurred since the booming era of the locomotives. More efficient diesel locomotives have replaced the steam-powered engines of the past. The Union Pacific Railroad Company has since acquired the Southern Pacific Railroad. Many of the historic depots are gone or have been put to other uses by their communities. The 1912 Roseburg Depot has been converted into a restaurant that still displays many relics and pictures from the days when railroads reigned in Douglas County.

Adventures in Railroading

Despite all the fascination with locomotives, railroading was a demanding job that required skill and a constant attention to detail. There was an unyielding dedication to the job and to co-workers. George Abdill eloquently describes the life of a railroader:

> Railroading is more than just a job...it is an undefinable substance that attaches itself to a man in so strong a manner that he is scarcely ever able to free himself from its grasp. It's a dog's life and men curse it, for it tears them from their homes and loved ones, demanding service in the black of the night when most civilized people are snugly abed. It is nerve-racking and exacting... not a man in train service that has not known fear when a foot stumbles or a mitt slips on a grab-iron while the rolling wheels grind underfoot; enginemen know the clutch at the heart when the monster machine they command bears down upon the heedless or unwitting...Railroading is the beat of the driving rain and the numb chill of wading through hip-deep snow; the red glow of caboose stoves when the wind howls around the cupola and the air in the "crummy" is thick with the aroma of strong coffee brewing over a coal fire, blue with tobacco smoke and the fumes of oil lamps...

Notwithstanding their best efforts, train derailments and accidents did occur. One unfortunate accident occurred on October 6, 1896. It involved a collision killing three men and injuring four others. After heading south out of Roseburg, a conductor realized he had forgotten his briefcase. He instructed the engineer to cut the engine and head back to the depot. Almost simultaneously, a Roseburg dispatcher who realized the conductor's mistake sent a light engine south to catch the train and deliver the briefcase at its scheduled stop in Myrtle Creek. A head-on crash between the north- and southbound trains occurred on a curve south of Green.

After an investigation, the board of inquiry determined the light engine had the right of way. The locomotive returning under the "flag" had the responsibility of seeing that the way was clear. In their haste to return for the briefcase, the conductor and engineer failed to adequately execute the "flagging" procedures. The rules called for a complete stop no less than half a mile from the curve, allowing a flagman to walk ahead and signal when the track was determined clear and passable. However, the conductor had pulled to within one hundred yards of the curve before stopping. The light engine went around the blind curve and immediately struck the engine.

ALONG THE RIVER

Umpqua River Lighthouses

In 1840, upon assessing the dangers of crossing the Umpqua River Bar, the Reverend Jason Lee recorded in his journal, "There is a bar at the mouth of the river, which I judge no ship can pass. The immense hills or mountains, which close in so closely upon the river as to leave it but just room to pass, are covered with dense forests to the water's edge…[the] whole region is gloomy and lonesome."

The entrance to the Umpqua River was unstable with the ocean currents flowing inward where the river made a sharp turn at Winchester Bay. Coupled with the tides and variable winds was the presence of hazardous sand bars along the river's bottom. The crossing for schooners over the bar was precarious at best.

On August 4, 1850, the schooner *Samuel Roberts* made a safe passage under the guidance of a whaleboat that included two local Indian guides.

Umpqua Lighthouse and coast guard buildings, circa 1890s. *Photo courtesy of the Douglas County Museum.*

The *Bostonian* was not so fortunate when it foundered while crossing the bar two months later. Joseph Lane, who was the Oregon Territory delegate to Congress, was allotted money to put in light signals and buoys near the mouth of the river. As more vessels were lost in the succeeding years, measures needed to be taken to replace the unreliable lights and buoys.

Congress eventually secured funding for a lighthouse that was completed in 1857. The sixty-four-foot Umpqua Lighthouse was the first of its kind on the Oregon Coast. The first light keeper, Fayette Crosby, tended to the lighthouse, which was built on the sand along the shore. However, the flood of 1860–61 caused significant damage to the integrity of the foundation, and in 1863 the unthinkable happened: it collapsed and toppled into the Umpqua River. The lens and lantern were salvaged from the rubble.

Mariners would have to wait until 1894, when a new sixty-five-foot-tall lighthouse was commissioned for service. The new lighthouse beacon reached approximately twenty miles out to sea with over 200,000 candlepower. In 1977, the structure was placed on the National Register of Historic Places.

Currently, over a century later, the lighthouse towers 165 feet above sea level from a bluff above Winchester Bay. The lens continues to serve as a guide to passing ships, emitting a white and red color sequence consisting of twelve rotating beams. Visitors can tour the lighthouse, and there is now a museum on the grounds in the historic coast guard station.

Navigating the Umpqua River

As the economy and agriculture grew in the interior valley of Douglas County, the farmers and businessmen began seeking a quicker, more reliable mode of transportation to get their goods to market. They were frustrated with the Drain-to-Scottsburg Road, which was narrow and often muddy.

A group of investors formed a stock company in 1869 called the Merchants and Farmers Navigation Company. The goal of the company was to secure a ship capable of navigating the Umpqua River to Roseburg and eventually on to Canyonville during months with higher water levels. A small sternwheeler, the *Swan*, was built by Hiram Doncaster in Gardiner. It was capable of carrying one hundred tons of cargo while drawing only thirteen inches of water. The March 6, 1870 Roseburg *Plaindealer* described the ship, "She is one hundred feet in length, twenty feet wide, and three and a half feet depth of hold inside the keel. Her engine is fifty horsepower."

The vessel, navigated by Captain Nicholas Haun, began its initial voyage in January 1870. Shortly after departing Scottsburg, the ship encountered rocks in Sawyers Rapids and broke both rudders. The crew repaired the rudders, and on February 10 the voyage continued, this time breaking only one rudder. The crew had to resort to using winches and pry bars in shallow areas, but the excitement built as the ship continued to make progress.

Entire communities lined the river to witness the progress. The *Swan* stopped in several places along the route to give onlookers rides aboard the boat. There is even mention of dancing aboard the ship on an overnight stop at Smith's Ferry. The ship commenced to blow its whistle as it rounded the bend at Roseburg on a Sunday morning. Churches emptied as residents headed to the riverside. Church bells rang, and firearms were discharged amid the cheering crowds. The water flow was considered too low, so they did not attempt to continue on to Canyonville via the South Umpqua River.

In July 1870, the Merchant and Farmers Navigation Company hired two engineers to study the feasibility of commercial navigation on the river. They confirmed that if they blasted a channel and removed other obstacles, it would allow for safe navigation for about seven months of the year. The costs of these improvements would be less than the costs incurred in one year of shipping the cargo on the overland route.

The United States Congress approved $22,600 for improvements to be made along the river. Thereafter, the new steamboat *Enterprise* attempted to navigate the Umpqua River, but it failed to get above Sawyers Rapids. There was never another successful trip made by any stern-wheeler between Scottsburg and Roseburg. In 1872, the Oregon & California Railroad arrived, providing a much more reliable and cheaper method of transporting goods to market.

School Boats on the Smith River

The rugged mountainous terrain in much of Douglas County has provided challenges for transportation. Rivers and streams often impeded the way for roads into remote villages. The costs of building bridges and grading the steep terrain for roads further hampered progress into these areas. With the lack of dependable roads, rural areas often resorted to small, one-room schoolhouses that taught primarily elementary grades. These areas had limited resources and availability for students to continue on through high school.

To provide an education for their children, families along the Smith River, under the direction of Noah and Gertrude Black, worked to open the Smith River School in 1921. This new school housed both elementary and high school grades. They contracted with a navigation company from Reedsport to carry students and teachers by boat ten miles up and down the river to school.

In 1926, Lorena Fisher had graduated from Linfield College in McMinnville and began fielding offers to become a high school teacher. She had entertained offers from small towns in Washington and Oregon but was hopeful for something "more interesting." Eventually, her tennis coach Maurice Pettit, who was leaving Linfield to become the principal at the Smith River School, offered Lorena a "unique" job teaching there. "This sounded adventurous to me, so I accepted on the spot," noted Lorena. One can't help but laugh at her next admission: "My parents didn't share my enthusiasm."

Lorena, who hadn't strayed too far from home before then, was driven by her brother in the family Model-T Touring Car from her home in McMinnville to Reedsport in early September 1926. She recalled Reedsport

The Smith River school boat *Bonita* loaded with schoolchildren in 1922. *Photo courtesy of the Douglas County Museum.*

as being small, with wooden plank streets built above the mud flats. It was susceptible to flooding, so small boats were available for use to get around town. "In those days it was a logging and dairy town...with an excellent creamery," observed Lorena.

At the waterfront in Reedsport, her possessions were loaded onto a boat for the short ride upriver to her new home. Fisher admitted, "I was beginning to wonder what I had gotten myself into." She stayed in an upstairs room at the home of Mary and Harry Marks and their two sons. The amenities included hot and cold running water but no electricity. Light was provided with kerosene and Aladdin lamps. There was a hand-crank telephone, which was on a party line with fifteen to twenty families. Harry Marks didn't want a "privy" inside the house, so an outhouse toilet was located a "respectable distance" out back.

Lorena rode the *Bonita*, which left Reedsport at 7:00 a.m. and crisscrossed the river picking up students at docks along the way. She was part of a group of six people who boarded from a dock, all carrying their lunches. There was no cafeteria at the school. Lorena described the boats as "large and comfortable with heated cabins in which the smaller grade school pupils were required to sit. The high school and upper-grade students were a bit freer to ride where they wished." One of her duties, along with the older students, was to look after the smaller children, making sure they didn't fall into the river.

The *Vulcan*, a double-decker boat, left a dock near Sulphur Springs and picked up students who lived along the upper river. Along with students, it carried mail and supplies for farms and logging camps along the river. The boats arrived at school around 9:00 a.m.

As for the high school curriculum, principal Pettit taught math, science and physical education. Lorena taught social studies, English and even a French class for this rural school with an enrollment of approximately fifty students. The small high school also had both girls' and boys' basketball teams that became archrivals with Reedsport.

After her second year of teaching at Smith River, Lorena accepted a job as principal at a small high school near Aberdeen, Washington. Eventually, the Smith River High School consolidated with Reedsport in 1944. Later in 1946, the elementary school joined with Gardiner. The Smith River school building was demolished. The gymnasium was sold to Noah Black, who had it dismantled and moved to his ranch near Eslick Creek, where he reassembled it in 1951.

Today, the Lower Smith River Road connects with Highway 101 just north of Reedsport. A scenic drive parallels the river for approximately twelve miles to the Riverside boat ramp. Near the entrance, a sign marks the historical point where the Smith River School once stood. Weathered posts standing along the river's edge are all that remain of the large school dock where the *Bonita* and the *Vulcan* once transported students to and from school.

In 1926, Lorena Stallings Fisher sought out a unique and adventurous teaching opportunity. She arrived in a rugged, untamed corner of Douglas County along the Smith River. The school boats era depicts a time and place unlike any other in the county's history.

4
Our Towns

There is an interesting parallel in how settlements became established as a city or town in Douglas County. The age-old expression "location, location, location" certainly makes up a key component in the equation of a town's significance. Most settlements were located near a natural resource, for employment in industries like timber, mining or farming. An early importance of proximity to rivers and river crossings for reliable transportation would later yield to the juxtaposition between towns and railroads. In some cases, a municipality's future livelihood came down to a matter of a few votes on where to run the tracks or road. The longevity of a settlement can also be traced to the resources and marketplace. A need for many of the area's industries and services, such as mines and ferries, have come and gone with the times. Some cities have managed to overcome and adapt to the changing climate of commerce, while some have been reduced to a skeleton version of their past and still others are but a distant memory.

The Western Front

Gardiner

On October 1, 1850, the *Bostonian*, captained by George Snelling, entered the harbor at the mouth of the Umpqua River. The ship, which had sailed around Cape Horn, floundered while attempting to cross the treacherous Umpqua Bar. The crew managed to salvage most of the cargo aboard the ship and carried it upriver to a site on a beach. They named the site Gardiner after the Boston merchant who owned most of the cargo.

With its placement along the shipping lines from San Francisco, this port town grew rapidly with homes and businesses. The Gardiner Mill Company was a major lumber mill in the region. Steamboats were also manufactured in the town. Early resident Alfred Reed hauled freight and passengers on the steamboat *Restless* from Scottsburg to Winchester Bay. From here, his brother Westley delivered the passengers and mail to Coos Bay on beach stagecoaches.

A tugboat with two schooners approaching Gardiner Mill. *Photo courtesy of the Douglas County Museum.*

Alfred was instrumental in developing Gardiner. He established the cannery operations on Cannery Island and also raised cattle for his meat market. He and his brother Wes operated a creamery and dairy that furnished milk and cream for the town. A fire on July 26, 1881, destroyed thirty-nine homes and businesses. The entire town was then reconstructed with all the buildings painted white, earning it the name "White City."

Alfred Reed was elected state senator in 1898, but tragically he drowned in the North Umpqua River near Winchester in 1899 while scouting a site for a salmon hatchery. His nephew Warren Reed inherited his estate and established Reedsport in Alfred's honor. Today, with most of its industry gone, Gardiner remains as a quaint tourist stop along Highway 101.

Reedsport

Reedsport was established when the Pacific Great Western Railroad Company constructed the Eugene–Coos Bay line. Warren Reed, who was heir to Alfred Reed's real estate and commercial holdings, owned much of the land through which the railroad passed. In all, Warren owned four thousand acres along the shore between the Umpqua River and Winchester Bay. The town was named in Alfred Reed's honor, and it was incorporated in 1919. Arguably, one of Reedsport's most famous citizens was Robin Reed, who won an Olympic Gold Medal in wrestling at the 1924 summer games in Paris.

With rail connections to both the Willamette Valley and towns along the coast, Reedsport became a viable shipping hub. The town was built in a low-lying area and was susceptible to flooding. It was first developed with elevated boardwalks along the banks of the Rainbow Slough. Most buildings were also elevated three to four feet above ground level along the wooden plank streets.

The city grew with the advancement of the railroads, and it elected Warren Reed as mayor. Reedsport was a logging town with two sawmills, a creamery and several canneries. The Rainbow was a popular restaurant in the 1920s, located near Burdick's Pharmacy. The town eventually filled in the low-lying areas and the slough with sand for a level business center. With the arrival of Highway 101, Reedsport opened more restaurants and motels to serve the tourists. Nearby Winchester Bay opened the Salmon Harbor Marina for boating, fishing and riding the sand dunes.

Reedsport's waterfront along the Rainbow Slough, circa 1920s. *Photo courtesy of the Douglas County Museum.*

Scottsburg

Scottsburg was the first town site to be surveyed and platted in either Umpqua or Douglas County. It was established by Levi Scott (a member of the Applegate Party) in 1850. Located at the end of the tidewaters, Scottsburg was a bustling shipping port of the day. However, the town was isolated from the remainder of the county by mountains until a military wagon road was completed between Myrtle Creek and Scottsburg. This allowed for supplies to be transported between the navigable portions of the Umpqua River to the Rogue River Valley via Myrtle Creek. Jacksonville merchants celebrated the road: "The wagon road is now opened between Jacksonville (via Myrtle Creek) and Scottsburg...packers are throwing away their pack saddles and purchasing wagons knowing they can haul cheaper than they can pack."

However, by the late 1850s the shipping industry in Scottsburg began to fade as ports in Crescent City, California, and Coos Bay were more easily accessible. The crippling floodwaters of 1861 destroyed Levi Scott's sawmill and all but wiped out Lower and Upper Scottsburg.

The stern-wheeler *Eva* on the Umpqua River, circa 1884. It was a mail and passenger boat from Scottsburg to Gardiner and Winchester Bay. *Photo courtesy of the Douglas County Museum.*

The resilient town made a comeback in 1876, when the Drain–Scottsburg stage began. The town was rejuvenated as the hub for the stages and stern-wheelers carrying passengers over the route between Drain and Coos Bay. The arrival of the railroad from Eugene to Coos Bay would draw a close to the stage route. Today, the picturesque town along the Umpqua River is a popular spot for tourists traveling on State Highway 38 to and from the coast or for some recreation at the nearby Loon Lake Resort.

NORTH COUNTY

Elkton

The Umpqua Land Company had planned to plat a town on a site where several Indian trails converged. However, when they passed the Donation Land Act in September 1850, the territory legislature prevented companies

A railroad surveying crew outside Weatherly's Eating House in Elkton in 1907. It was a popular lunch stop on the Drain–Scottsburg stage line. *Photo courtesy of the Douglas County Museum.*

and nonresidents from obtaining public lands for speculation. The land became the property of James Levins, who acquired a 640-acre land claim along Elk Creek. His claim was adjacent to the Hudson's Bay Company's Fort Umpqua, which had been in the area for fifteen years. Levin in turn donated 160 acres of his claim to the newly established Umpqua County. The land was surveyed and platted, and in 1851 Elkton became the county seat of Umpqua County.

Farmer Henry Beckley organized a capital company and built a sawmill and flour mill in the town. He would later be elected to the Oregon House of Representatives. When Umpqua dissolved into Douglas County, he twice represented Douglas County in the senate.

Elkton became a main stop for the Drain–Scottsburg stage line. This was largely due to the popularity of Weatherly's Eating House. Charlie Weatherly was an extraordinary cook, and the stagecoaches timed their routes both ways to arrive in Elkton at lunchtime. While the relay horses were changed out at the Elkton livery, the patrons were treated to some fine dining. Charlie learned to cook by default. His sister Elle, who was entrusted with the kitchen work, despised housework, so she and Charlie began switching chores.

A couple fires in the early 1900s destroyed most of the town, including Weatherly's Hotel and Eating House. Today, the small town still serves travelers with a couple fine restaurants and a general store. Families enjoy the Elkton Butter Fly Garden Pavilion and walks around the historic Fort Umpqua grounds.

Drain

Warren Goodell settled on a land claim in the Drain locale in 1847. In 1861, Charles Drain bought the land and platted the town site. Drain was situated on the crossroads of an overland stage that linked Jacksonville and the Willamette Valley. Charles Drain saw the potential in the railroad and sold the Oregon & California Railroad sixty acres for one dollar. The railroad brought prosperity to the town, and plans were made to continue the rails to the coast. However, after a substantial investment by the railroad company, an alternative route was chosen from Eugene. The Drain–Scottsburg Stage Road did mature, beginning service in 1876.

The Elk Creek Tunnel between Drain and Elkton was constructed in 1931. At almost 1,200 feet long, it was a major engineering achievement for transportation between Reedsport and Curtin. So important was the tunnel that it was considered a strategic point to be guarded during World War II. Betty Kruse Smith explains, "Holes were bored into the walls, and in case of invasion, dynamite sticks would be placed in the holes and set to explode." There was also a machine gun nest near the east side of the tunnel.

The stagecoaches of the past that once crisscrossed Drain were eventually phased out. At present, the sleepy logging town remains as part of a main thoroughfare between Interstate 5 and Reedsport.

Yoncalla

When establishing their trail, the Applegate Party passed through the Yoncalla Valley in June 1846. As they rode their horses along the Halo Indian Trail, they were fascinated by the beauty of the tall grasses and streams. They vowed to return and settle on land claims there after completing the Applegate Trail.

The "Drain Castle," built by Charles Drain in the 1890s, demonstrates the Queen Ann architectural style. The cost of the house was estimated at $2,600. *Sketch drawn by Lauretta Kaderlik.*

The first settlers to the area were Robert Cowan and his family, who built a log cabin in 1848. The following year, Jesse Applegate took a claim near Mount Yoncalla with his extended family, including his daughter Rozelle and her husband, Charles Putnam. Putnam edited a newspaper called the *Oregon American and Evangelican Unionist* and taught Rozelle the trade; she then became the first female typesetter in Oregon.

Jesse Applegate named the town Yoncalla, which he interpreted as the Indian word for eagles. He established a small store in town and served as the first postmaster. Robert Booth was also an early merchant and sawmill owner. Caleb Tracy ran an apparel store featuring ladies' and men's wear. Tracy's was the place where residents gathered for coffee and to keep up on the local gossip and politics. Charles Applegate owned a blacksmith shop. Between the years 1852 and 1856, he built a house outside Yoncalla where he and his wife, Melinda, raised sixteen children. The house is called the divided house—half for men and half for women. The house remains in the family today.

The Applegate House built by Charles and Melinda Applegate in the 1850s. It currently serves as the headquarters for the Heritage Arts and Education Organization. *Photo courtesy of the Douglas County Museum.*

The city benefitted over the years by being on the Oregon and California Stage Road as well as the railroad. The popularity of the nearby Boswell Hot Springs Resort brought additional traffic to Yoncalla. Prunes were grown and dried in the area. Earnest Warner had a prune dryer at his place along Highway 99, where many tourists stopped to observe the operation.

CENTRAL CITIES

Oakland

A stroll through the quaint downtown of Oakland is like watching the pages of history unfold before your eyes. Joseph Cornwall and his family arrived in the valley in 1846. Exhausted from the long journey along the Applegate Trail, he built a cabin for his family to recuperate and to protect his library of books. In 1851, Dr. Dorsey Baker arrived and established Old Town Oakland, where he built a gristmill on the Calapooia Creek.

The old town expanded until news that the Oregon & California Railroad planned to run tracks about a mile south of town. This led to a relocation effort by Alonzo Brown, who in 1872 established the present-day town site adjacent to the railroad. The new town thrived with a mercantile, tavern and stagecoach line. By the turn of the twentieth century, Oakland was a large processor of turkeys.

After experiencing two major fires in 1892 and 1899, the Oakland residents made a wise decision to rebuild their buildings with brick. Many of these buildings remain in use today. The second floor of the 1890 Page and Dimmick Building was used by Dr. Page while the lower floor was a pharmacy. The Oakland Museum occupies the building that housed the Underwood Red and White Mercantile. Next door, the Medley Building offered the first limelight projector movies in Oakland.

The historic tavern has been serving patrons since 1898. Opened in 1891, Stearns and Chenoweth Hardware, which once sold a wide variety of merchandise such as buggies, wagons and sewing machines, continues today as a hardware store operated by the Stearns family. The Smith Livery Stable, established in 1884, still stands on the corner of Third and Locust.

Today, a self-guided tour of downtown Oakland brings one back to earlier times. Tolly's restaurant serves old-fashioned ice cream sodas in one of the city's landmark buildings once known as Mode's Emporium.

Sutherlin

John F. Sutherlin and his family arrived in the valley known as Camas Swale in 1851 from Greencastle, Indiana. John and his wife, Sarah, who had ten children, were wealthy. They brought almost $30,000 with them across the Oregon Trail. John made loans to other settlers with a high return on the 25 percent interest rate he charged. He also established a sawmill and was a successful rancher. In 1883, his son Fendal was the wealthiest resident in Douglas County. The town was incorporated and named after the Sutherlin family in 1911.

Fendal's daughter Annie married Frank Waite, and they joined Henry Luce to form the Luce Land Company. The company sold small parcels of

The home built by early settler John R. Sutherlin in 1906. The town of Sutherlin was named after the Sutherlin family. *Photo courtesy of the Douglas County Museum.*

orchard land in the valley, from five to twenty acres. They advertised that growing fruit in the fertile valley was a safe investment. However, in the end, the Luce Land Company and many landowners would go bankrupt.

The timber industry, however, was a successful mainstay for Sutherlin, as the town experienced a boom in its population and economy in the 1940s. With the arrival of the railroad, the city built a connecting rail to haul logs from the Roach Timber Unit to the main line of the Southern Pacific Railroad.

Roseburg

The area of present-day Roseburg was originally known as Deer Creek for its location on the confluence of the South Umpqua River and Deer Creek. Merchant Aaron Rose and his wife, Sarah, arrived in the valley on the Applegate Trail. They filed for a donation land claim (a squatters' rights claim) near this site on September 25, 1851. They opened a general store, a tavern and a butcher shop, along with a successful business that sold horses.

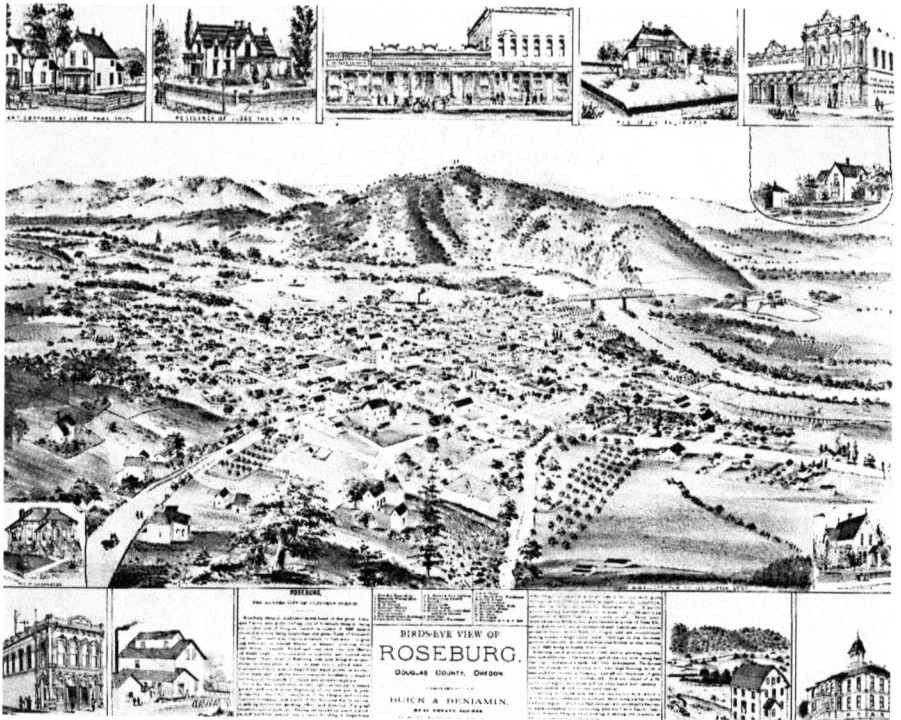

A bird's-eye view of Roseburg surrounded by pictures of prominent Roseburg buildings, circa July 1889. *Photo courtesy of the Douglas County Museum.*

Rose was well respected in the area and was elected to the territorial legislature. With ambitions for promoting his own town and business center, Rose succeeded in luring voters to choose Deer Creek as the county seat of the newly established Douglas County over the rival town of Winchester. To sweeten the deal, he offered three acres of land and $1,000 toward the construction of the county's courthouse building. The growing town site was eventually named Roseburgh in 1857 and later changed to Roseburg in 1894.

With a keen sense of foresight, the visionary Aaron Rose saw the potential in a proposed wagon road to open an overland route from the port of Coos Bay (Marshfield) through the nearby town of Lookingglass in Douglas County. According to documents at the Douglas County Museum, Rose was an eager investor in the Coos Bay Wagon Road Company. His instincts proved correct, as the Roseburgh area flourished, serving as the terminus of both the Wagon Road and the railroad in 1872. Perhaps not as successful in his personal life, Aaron Rose was married four times before he died in March 1899.

Today, Roseburg serves as the western gateway to Crater Lake National Park while maintaining its title "Timber Capital of the Nation."

SOUTH COUNTY

Canyonville

The town of Canyonville is located at a natural hub at the confluence of the South Umpqua River with both Canyon Creek and Cow Creek. The stages and railroads have taken advantage of this convenient stop at the base of several southern Oregon mountain passes. Travelers along the Applegate Trail secured provisions here, and gold prospectors purchased supplies before heading their pack trains east to the Coffee Creek mines.

Jackson Reynolds settled on the initial land claim along Canyon Creek in 1851, eventually selling the land to Jesse Roberts. After platting the site, Roberts named the town Canyonville. He constructed a gristmill and the Robert's Hotel.

From 1879 to 1882, Jerome Sullivan served as the keeper of the gate at a controversial tollgate at a bridge on Canyon Creek, south of Canyonville. Although it was a small toll, it infuriated Hardy Elliff, who is reported to have thrown the tollgate into the creek. There was a lawsuit filed that went all the way to the Oregon Supreme Court. The suit was brought by the Douglas County Road Company against Solomon Abraham and others involved with charging tolls. The court ruled that the route extended along a public highway and the defendants had obstructed "said road" by erecting a tollgate thereon. "The Plaintiff could use all bridges along the line of road as far as they can be made available."

Tragedy struck on January 16, 1974, when nine men working to repair a phone line south of Canyonville were killed in a massive landslide on Canyon Mountain. Seven were employees of the Pacific Northwest Bell Company relay station, and two worked for a Gold Hill contractor. There is a memorial to these men at Stanton Park in North Canyonville.

Main Street Canyonville looking north in 1910. *Photo courtesy of the Douglas County Museum.*

Canyonville continues to serve as a stop for travelers along Interstate 5. The Seven Feathers Casino attracts over a million visitors to the city annually.

Glendale

Glendale was not incorporated until 1901. However, by the early 1880s, major growth came to this logging town with the expansion of the Oregon–California Railroad. Early settlers like William Juyler, Lorenzo Montgomery and Solomon Abraham realized its potential for timber. Abraham platted the site and named it Julia, after his wife.

The post office made the town name official when it opened shop in February 1883. However, when the railroad arrived, to the surprise of the settlers, it placed the name "Glendale" on the train depot. A dispute ensued between Abraham and Charles Morris of the Oregon & California Railroad. On August 23, 1883, the decision was final, and the town was then Glendale. Despite the name change, the town expanded quickly with the construction of the Palace Hotel, several stores and, in 1901, the Glendale Lumber Company.

In 1890, Glendale endured a terrible winter with over seven feet of snow. The town was isolated as train service and mail came to a halt. Cattle and

Members of the Glendale band taken in downtown Glendale in 1908. *Photo courtesy of the Douglas County Museum.*

wildlife died as a result of the snow, and in the spring, melting snow brought floods and landslides. Then there was the fire of 1911. In less than an hour after the city hall bell alarm, most of the town lay in smoldering ruins. Residents fought the fire with hoses, but due to a conservation effort by the city, the water pressure had been turned to low.

A proud moment for the community was in 1915, when Kathryn Clarke was elected from Glendale as Oregon's first female senator. Her family owned and operated a hotel in town. Although still a logging town, Glendale slowed considerably when it was bypassed by Interstate 5.

A SIGN OF THE TIMES

Kellogg

Nestled in a valley along a bend in the North Umpqua River, approximately six miles south of the town of Elkton, a signpost marks the spot where John Jay Kellogg and his family settled in 1849. John, along with his two sons

The extended Kellogg family. The town of Kellogg was named in honor of John Jay Kellogg, the first white settler. *Photo courtesy of the Douglas County Museum.*

Lyman and Adna "Barnes," laid claim to bottomland within a crescent formed by the river. The crescent was referred to as *Chinagouche* by local Indians. With its fertile soil and lush grasses, the area had also garnered names such as Sheep Heaven and Pleasant Plain.

In the early 1850s, other settlers arrived in the area to stake their claims as well. On February 26, 1856, a United States Post Office was established there. John Jay Kellogg was appointed postmaster for the town named Kellogg in his honor. The Kelloggs built a gristmill on the Umpqua River at the mouth of McGee Creek. However, in July 1857, John Kellogg fell while working on the mill and drowned in the river. His sons continued to operate the mill until it was destroyed in the flood of 1861. Lyman Kellogg would also replace John as postmaster. He lived in the area for thirty years, before moving to Oakland after the death of his wife, Mary. Barney's Peak got its name from Adna Barnes Kellogg. Adna, who never married, lived in the Kellogg area his entire life. The Diamond "C" ranch is now located on his original land claim.

Kellogg, due to its location in the valley, was part of a well-traveled route between Sutherlin and Elkton. To accommodate the travelers, including mail carriers, ferries were necessary for the safe crossing of the river. In 1852, Edward Drew operated the Crescent Ferry across the Umpqua River, where the Highway 138 Bridge crosses today. The ferry, which changed names and owners over the years, continued to run until Douglas County bought the Dimmick and Fryer Ferry (named for Kellogg settlers Zeba Dimmick and John Fryer) in 1910. The bridge replaced the ferry in 1914.

With the advent of roads and bridge crossings, Kellogg became less significant to travelers, and the population dwindled along with its commerce. In 1921, the post office was closed. The Grange building still remains among the pastoral ranches where the once-thriving town of Kellogg stood.

Lookingglass in the National Spotlight

Hoy Flournoy was an early settler in the area who founded the French settlement (the present-day town of Melrose). In 1846, while out exploring and surveying the surrounding area, he came across a beautiful valley where "the light reflected off the tall, green, green grass like a mirror." Hoy would name the valley Lookingglass.

By the 1870s, the village was bustling with activity. The Lookingglass Store stood at a junction that served as the terminus for the Oakland–Lookingglass Stage and as the eastern starting point for the Coos Bay Wagon Road. The post office was established there in 1871. In addition to the store, there was also a livery stable and a nearby saloon. A grange hall was added in 1898. However, this was near the end of the height of activity in Lookingglass. Eventually, the stage lines were replaced by automobiles. The town is off the beaten path of the interstate and highways. Today, the historical general store is still the heart of Lookingglass. There is evidence of the mail slot on the front of the building, although the post office was removed in 1942. Just outside town, along the Coos Bay Wagon Road, is the James Wimer Octagonal Barn. Built in 1892, the barn is listed on the National Register of Historical Places.

In 1970, Mayor Norm Nibblett had a keen sense of humor about the small town. He installed a two-horse parking meter next to the store. The meter was donated by Roseburg with an official ceremony. Roseburg mayor Joe Boatright not only donated the meter but also appointed Nibblett the honorary meter maid and justice for meter enforcement in Lookingglass. Nibblett planned to use the proceeds from the "voluntary" meter to pay for a water trough.

The Lookingglass Store and service station. The general store is still the hub of the community today. *Photo courtesy of the Douglas County Museum.*

This grabbed national attention, and Charles Kuralt paid a visit for his *On the Road* segment for CBS. David Brinkley appeared on the NBC *Nightly News* from the steps of the store as well. Ironically, Brinkley's co-anchor, Chet Huntley of the *Huntley-Brinkley Report*, was the great-grandson of David Huntley, an early settler in Lookingglass.

On July 13, 1971, the town installed its first telephone booth at the north end of the store. Norm Nibblett declared, "We now have a parking meter at one end of town and phone booth at the other." The meter was located at the north end of the store and the booth on the south side. Right on cue, the phone rang during the dedication. Excitedly, Nibblett answered the call, which—as it turned out—was the wrong number. They've since added a fire hydrant and two manhole covers that cover nothing. Both covers were donated to the town. One came from the mayor of Cedar Rapids, Iowa, and the other from an iron company in Eugene.

Although parking was free, tourists and locals still plugged the meter. Nibblett recalled, "One day a teen boy was standing on the front porch [of the store] watching the meter. I asked what was wrong? The boy replied, 'I got twelve minutes [left on the meter] so I want to use it all up.'"

Tiller & Drew

Nestled in the southeast corner of Douglas County, Tiller was named for Aaron Tiller, an early settler in the area. He and his wife, Rachel Amanda Tiller, homesteaded just above the present-day town site. Rachel served as postmistress of the Elk Creek post office, which was later moved to Tiller. At one time, the town had a hotel along with a store. The hotel has since burned down. The Rondeau family built a schoolhouse around 1905. Floyd Watson served as the first teacher.

Today, the current Tiller store is operated by Erika and Ed Carlyle. Erika displays pictures of the local history complete with captions. She especially enjoys seeing the children take interest in their history. The area history includes gold mining on Coffee Creek along the Russell Gulch, where gold was first discovered in 1852. The historic Tiller Ranger Station was built for the U.S. Forest Service by the Civilian Conservation Corps' (CCC) Company 2904 in the 1930s.

Drew, which is several miles east of Tiller, is said to be named after Robert Drew. It was primarily a logging town. The post office was established in 1902, and in 1915 the community added a public school. Both have

The Tiller Store in 1811. The store is a chinked-log structure. Shown are members of the Rondeau family. Tom Rondeau is pictured on the porch in the upper right-hand corner. *Photo courtesy of the Douglas County Museum.*

been discontinued. Today, a spot marking "Downtown Drew, Oregon," is displayed at a residence along a row of homes.

A State of Mind

The Lone Rock Free State

The Colliding Rivers near Glide was a summer camp for the Umpqua Indians. In 1890, the Wrights and Shrums settled in the area. In fact, the first reported school was on the Shrum place on Little River Road near Buckhorn Road. Glide was also the site of an important east–west crossing of the North Umpqua River via the Lone Rock Ferry.

The post office was without a name until, one day, postmistress Virginia Laird's son came home singing the song "The River Goes Gliding Along." The post office, and therefore the town, had a name. East of Glide on

Picture from a souvenir postcard from the Peel Store depicting friends celebrating the "Days of 1849." Dated 1895. *Photo courtesy of the Douglas County Museum.*

Highway 138 is the town of Idleyld Park. It originally began in 1920 as an amusement park.

South of Glide on the Little River Road, A.A. Engels and his son Lafe built a store on their timber claim near the Cavitt Creek. A schoolhouse was built next to the store. The town was named Peel after a state representative they knew in Arkansas. The store housed a post office, and it was part of a stagecoach line on a route with stops at Roseburg, Oak Creek, Glide and Peel. The Through Stage Line offered early travelers a "Fancy Facility to the Lone Rock Free State Area." The fees began at fifty cents and went up to one dollar for the entire ride from Roseburg to Peel, a distance of 24.5 miles. A short-lived town was built on Cavitt Creek called No Fog. It was built primarily for mining purposes and for the Chinese laborers working on the China Ditch.

No Fog has long been abandon, and there is another Peel Store down the road from the original village. Glide maintains a post office, a general store and a U.S. Forest Service office. The historic Glide Ranger Station, built in 1938 by the CCC, remains open to the public. Idleyld Park and nearby Steamboat offer world-class fly-fishing.

New Odessa: A Communal Experiment

Little was known at the time about a group of Jewish immigrants who had purchased 760 acres near Julia (present-day Glendale) in the spring of 1883. This led locals to refer to it as the "Ghost Community." The group, which referred to itself as Am Olem (the eternal people), had escaped persecution in Russia and immigrated to the United States. The group bought the land, which contained two homes, for $4,800, with a down payment of $2,000. The rest of the balance was due in installments over the next few years. About three-quarters of the land was forest, while the remainder was farmable acreage.

Paul Kaplan is said to have been the original leader of the assembly of intellectuals who named the town New Odessa in honor of their previous home in Russia. The town was in actuality an experimental commune. The separatists all lived upstairs in one of the houses while the downstairs was used for cooking, dining and meetings. Their desire was to live simply off the land. Their main recreational activities included debating, reading and dancing to Russian folk music. Dances were held in a hall that drew people from the surrounding communities. They grew large gardens. Vegetables, fruit and bread were the mainstays of their diet. Work was divided equally as men and women took turns in the forestry and household chores. In 1883, when William Frey moved with his family to the commune, he caused a division within the community. He preached his faith in the "Religion of Humanity" and his belief in "Positivism" to this non-religious group of Marxist thinkers.

A community member's letter from August 2, 1883, notes:

> *A month has passed since the arrival of the Frey family. Their coming regulated our spiritual life…On Monday, Tuesday, Thursday and Fridays we have mathematics and English and the philosophy of "Positivism" with William Frey.*

Besides farming, the community also sold wood to Harry Villard to use as ties for his railroad company. Some of the group's members also worked in the town of Julia. All of their earnings were put into a community fund. The colony's population reached approximately sixty-five people before unraveling.

There are many contending theories about the demise of New Odessa. In 1885, the differences between Frey and his followers versus Kaplan's disciples caused Frey and fifteen members to leave town. Also, the influx of cheaper Chinese laborers took away their timber sales. Other members simply sought more opportunities outside the small village for themselves and their children. In March 1887, the community was served foreclosure papers by Douglas County sheriff A.B. Agee. To his surprise, none of the defendants who had originated the land purchase and signed for the loan remained in the community. Over the years, the commune had made only a single payment of $100. There was no community fund to speak of and no forwarding addresses. Today, the "Ghost Community" of New Odessa has vanished and is now ranchland.

5

Notable Women

*Somewhere out in this audience may even be someone who will one day
follow in my footsteps and preside over the White House as the president's
spouse. I wish him well.*
—First Lady Barbara Bush

Throughout its history, Douglas County has had many notable women
who deserve recognition for their contributions to both our county and
state history. From the county's inception, many pioneer women quietly
labored long, hard hours maintaining households and raising families without
seeking or receiving any fanfare. Through their efforts, they provided the
backbone of stability that resonated throughout their communities.

PIONEERING EDUCATION AND HUMANITY

As part of the Great Migration in 1843, Melinda Applegate and her husband,
Charles, were among the first pioneers to locate in the area, settling in the
Yoncalla Valley. After their home was completed in 1856, they graciously
opened their doors to provide for neighbors as well as strangers who were
traveling through. Despite having sixteen children of their own, Melinda
took the time to teach Indian mothers modern techniques for raising

their children as well as the craft of making quilts. Being firm believers in education, she and Charles shipped an entire library of books from Harper's Publishing Company of New York to Yoncalla, and in 1851, they built the first schoolhouse in Douglas County on their property. James Applegate was installed as the teacher.

LADIES' FIRSTS

First Senator

Kathryn Clarke of Glendale was Oregon's first elected female senator in 1915. This was quite a feat when you take a closer look at that time period. The Nineteenth Amendment to the United States Constitution was not ratified until 1920. Women in Oregon had, however, achieved the right to vote in 1912, and they became eligible to serve in the Oregon Legislative Assembly by 1914.

In January 1915, Senator George Neuner Jr. resigned to become a district attorney. Governor Oswald West appointed his cousin Kathryn Clarke to fill the vacant senate seat. This led to a debate challenging the governor's authority to appoint someone to fill the position. Thus, when a special election was called, Kathryn threw her hat into the ring and filed as a Republican. History was made on January 20, 1915, when Douglas County voters elected Clarke—who won by a mere seventy-six votes. Recently in 2011, the Oregon legislature honored Clarke by naming a room adjacent to the Senate Chambers the Senator Kathryn Clarke Cloakroom.

First Autopsy

In a time when "the practice of medicine was thought unfit for a woman," Bethenia Owens-Adair overcame many obstacles to become a doctor at the age of forty. As was common in those days, she was married at age fourteen in 1854. Two years later, she gave birth to a son named George. Born in poor health, George was susceptible to crying often, for which her husband, Legrand, would severely punish him. When Bethenia protested, he turned

Bethenia Owens-Adair, the first female doctor to perform an autopsy in Oregon. *Photo courtesy of the Douglas Museum.*

his fury toward her. She was granted a divorce from her abusive husband at age eighteen.

As a single mother, she moved north to teach in Clatsop County. Owens-Adair returned to Roseburg to open a dressmaking and millinery shop. In her book *Women in Oregon*, Leona Johnson wrote, "By secretly watching her rival from a rooftop, she learned to bleach, block and press hats." She succeeded in the millinery business and had one of Roseburg's first show windows added to her shop.

Later, she attended the Eclectic School of Medicine in Philadelphia for a year. Returning home in 1874, she would become the first female doctor to perform an autopsy in Oregon. In 1880, Bethenia went on to earn her medical degree at the University of Michigan. After graduation, she worked at hospitals throughout Europe. Bothered by the stereotypes in medicine, Owens-Adair noted, "I had discovered in my work…that it is women who are the sufferers from bad laws, so I decided to dedicate my life to the securing of better laws and the creation of a sentiment against the double standard of morals."

First to Hold Public Office and Pioneer of Justice

The first woman to be elected to a public office in Douglas County was Agnes Pitchford, when she was elected as the Roseburg City treasurer in 1913. But Agnes was more readily known as a pioneer in the county juvenile justice system. In 1916, she began a career spanning fifty years as the director of the Douglas County Juvenile Department. Author Leona Johnson notes, "She traveled throughout the county by train until she acquired a Model-T Ford coupe. Travel was much slower before Highways 101 and 38 were completed, and it took "Aggie" several days to travel between Roseburg and Reedsport. She brought high boots to wear, as she had to walk several miles to homes in Winchester Bay. In the back of her car, she also carried a wooden pail filled with candy to treat the children along the way. At Christmas, the car was filled with gifts." Agnes retired in 1953 but continued to work part time as a counselor until 1966. The Pitchford Boy's Ranch, a facility for delinquent boys, was named in her honor. In 1964, she received the Oregon Juvenile Council Award for the outstanding service she provided.

First Teacher and Entrepreneur

Esther Selover Lockhart arrived in Oregon in 1851. She and her husband, Freeman, moved with their small child to the Camas Swale area of Douglas County in 1852. As they settled into their 320-acre land claim, the Lockharts lived out of a tent while building a cabin. The brilliant blue blossoms of the camas that blanketed the large meadows also served as cover for a large population of rattlesnakes in the area. One sunny afternoon, a large rattlesnake entered the tent and lay between Esther and her sleeping child. With great resolve, she killed the snake by grinding an axe on its head. It was indeed a large snake with seven rattles and a button.

When they finished the cabin, Mrs. Lockhart became quite an entrepreneur. "As many hungry travelers passed the Lockhart cabin, Esther began selling pies; 50 cents for custard, apple and peach and $1.00 for mincemeat. She also sold a piece of pie or little cakes with a glass of fresh milk. In two months she took in $300. For serving meals she earned $300 more." That was a tidy sum of money in those days.

In 1854, Esther and Freeman opened the first school in adjacent Coos County at Empire City. She taught five students in a small log shack, while Freeman served as the county's first school superintendant.

BRAVING THE ELEMENTS

Wrestling Cougars

For Sophia Ellen Tibbett McKinney, bravery against the elements was merely a means to survival. In 1852, she was just ten years old when her family made the long trip across country from Indiana to Oregon. From the time they were married in 1858, Sophia and her husband had lived in Washington and California before returning to homestead in Umpqua County, Oregon. They built a cabin with a large fireplace, and they raised hogs. One night, they heard a pig squealing. As Sophia recounted:

> *My husband grabbed his gun and told the hired man to bring the light so he could see to shoot the bear or cougar that was killing the pig. The hired man said it wasn't healthy to tackle a cougar after dark when they were eating, so I grabbed up the candle and went out to where the cougar was. My husband said, "Hold the light near him," so I held the candle bout six feet from him. My husband couldn't see the sights on his gun, so I stepped a little closer. This made the cougar provoked, so it jumped on me and rolled me over and over. Knocking me down that way put out the light, so the cougar got away.*

The cougar returned the next night, and her husband set the dogs on it. When it was cornered, he shot and killed it. The cougar that had attacked her the night before measured over ten feet long. Sophia then made a rug out of it.

Around the Campfire

Myrtle Creek was home to a delightful lady known as Aunt Phoebe Newton. She was reluctant to tell her story to Fred Lockley of the *Oregon Journal* and have her name right in the paper where everyone could see it. "Just the thought of it makes me break out in a sweat," she explained. "I have been here in or near Myrtle Creek for more than 65 years and I have never done anything yet to get my name in the papers."

But on an October day in 1930, Lockley succeeded in getting Phoebe to shed some light into her past.

> *Do I remember our trip across the plains? I should say I do. We started from Caldwell County, Missouri, in the spring of '64. I was a woman grown. I was upwards of 15 years old...We had four yoke of cattle on one wagon—three yoke of oxen and one yoke of cows. Both women and the cows had to work hard in those days. The cows not only furnished us milk but they had to help pull the wagon...that was 66 years ago...but I can shut my eyes and almost hear the songs we sang around the campfires made of sagebrush, cottonwood, or greasewood.*

CONSERVATION

Reggie Miller, along with Audrey Young and Mona Riley, started the Glide Wildflower Show in 1965 as a fundraising project. For the original show, Reggie is said to have collected 71 specimens of wildflowers in three days from around her home on Buckhorn Road. The show had an attendance of 38 people. By 1972, the show had grown to 380 species with 4,500 people attending.

Reggie and her husband, Raymond, moved to a 180-acre ranch near Glide on Buckhorn Road in 1954. She worked as a floral designer and was an expert on local wildflowers. In addition to her involvement in several civic organizations, she offered presentations on wildflowers to schools and garden clubs in the area, and in 1971 Reggie received the First Citizen Award for her contributions to the Glide community.

For her work in the conservation of wildflowers, Miller received awards from both the Roseburg District Federated Garden Club and the Oregon State Federated Garden Club.

The Glide Wildflower Show is not just about displaying wildflowers; it is also about the conservation of wildflowers. Reggie noted, "Wildflowers are often abundant, but they are not indestructible; many of our loveliest ones are in danger of extinction by our carelessness. By knowing our wildflowers, we can preserve them for ourselves and the future." The show, which continues to gain in popularity, currently runs the last weekend of April at the Glide Community Center. It now includes over six hundred species.

MILDRED KANIPE

In the 1870s, Thomas and Emily Baimbridge settled in an area east of Oakland, Oregon, with friends and relatives. The families named the area the English Settlement and built a school for their children. Thomas and Emily's youngest child, Sarah, was born in their home in 1876. She would later marry rancher John Kanipe. In February 1905, their first child, Leah Kathryn, was born. Two years later, in September 1907, another daughter, Mildred, was born. However, Sarah died later that same year, in December.

Soon after her death, Sarah's sister moved into the home to raise Mildred and Leah. Author Lois Christiansen Eagleton explains, "Mildred's full name is Mary Mildred Kanipe, but she never used her first name, perhaps because her mother's sister Mary moved in with the family after her mother died to take care of the household and raise the two girls."

Mildred loved living in the open spaces of the ranch. She never married, and she continued to work the ranch with her father. She herself bought an additional 167 acres nearby. When her father, John, died in 1940, he left each daughter a parcel of land. Mildred's inheritance included the English Settlement School, along with the house and barns on the ranch. In all, it totaled 290.77 acres.

Mildred Kanipe pictured with sheep on her ranch in the 1940s. *Photo courtesy of the Douglas County Museum.*

In addition to her love of the land, Mildred also loved animals, especially horses. On her land, she grew hay and raised chickens, sheep and goats. She also raised cattle on the ranch, and she established a successful dairy to supplement her income, along with selling the sheep's wool. In 1949, with the purchase of another ranch containing 633 acres, she now had 1,090.77 contiguous acres of ranchland to maintain. She managed the ranch with the help of her aunt Mary until Mary's death in 1955. After that, she hired ranch hands.

Mildred had been born in the home of her grandparents Thomas and Emily Baimbridge, which was part of her ranch. She took great pleasure in maintaining the ranch that had been in the family all those years. Upon her death on July 13, 1973, Mildred donated her ranch to Douglas County to be used as a park. She also left five acres within the city of Oakland for a park. She left strict conditions for preservation of the ranch land. The Mildred Kanipe Memorial Park has beautiful horse and hiking trails. Some of the original ranch buildings still stand today. Often, visitors to the park are initially greeted by the many splendid peacocks that reside there.

The Women of Yoncalla Rock the Vote

The events leading up to the memorable election in Yoncalla on November 2, 1920, had all the makings for an episode on *The Andy Griffith Show*. An uprising caused dissention in the sleepy town of Yoncalla between the local women and the all-male city council.

The ladies of Yoncalla were dissatisfied with what they considered the "inefficiency" of the mayor and his all-male city council. The town's sidewalks were in disrepair beneath the poorly lit streets. The municipality seemed to be tolerating motorists who sped through town. And if the stench of the local outhouses weren't enough, there were countless dogs running at large.

The ladies had reached a boiling point, and they began to meet independently to discuss their grievances. In a pre-election meeting, it was suggested that the women should take matters into their own hands and put their names on the ballot. And so, a new chapter was written in the halls of Yoncalla. Wilfred Brown wrote, "Two ladies filed for council seats, whereupon, all the male incumbents resigned their unpaid and largely thankless jobs."

The women would set precedence as they swept the entire municipal ticket and became the first all-female city government in America. Mary Burt was elected mayor. Her council members consisted of Nettie Hannan, Jennie D. Lasswell, Edith B. Thompson and Bernice Wilson. For the women of Oregon, voting had become a way of life since 1912. But voting had just been granted to most women in the country when the Nineteenth Amendment to the Constitution was ratified in that same year (1920). The news made headlines across the nation, and the now-famous ladies appeared in several news magazines.

6

Commerce

Throughout its history, the county has seen quite a variety of sectors in agriculture and industry. The fluctuation and changing landscape of the market for certain crops, livestock and commodities have led to several interesting peaks and valleys along the way.

AGRICULTURE

Cattle Drive

Early ranchers in the area found raising sheep for wool production to be a profitable venture. In 1865, Douglas County had over forty thousand sheep, which produced over 100,000 pounds of wool. With the plentiful grasses, the ranchers sought to further supplement their incomes by raising cattle, too. In 1837, former trapper Ewing Young was the leader of an expedition to drive cattle north from as far as Mexico and California to Douglas County. After an arduous trip, he delivered six hundred head of cattle, purchased for three dollars a head. Thus, cattle ranching became a way of life here.

Alfred Reed raised cattle on his property, known as "The Ranch," for his meat market in the Gardiner area. The Nichols Brothers Ranch near Winston became a large cattle operation. It was originally operated by James and Nancy Dalvin. When their daughter Ada married Israel Nichols, the place became known as the Nichols Ranch. Ada, a shrewd businesswoman, continued to develop the ranch, which she handed down to her sons, Syd and Harold. Syd ran the family's Brockway General Store, and Harold worked the ranch, which ultimately expanded into a dairy operation as well.

In the next generation, Dick Nichols incorporated the ranch in 1963. Under Dick's management, the Nichols Ranch would become one of the largest cattle operations in Oregon. However, as profits dwindled by the late 1990s, the corporation discontinued its cattle operations.

A Turkey Drive?

Fendel Sutherlin is credited with introducing turkeys to Douglas County in the 1850s. Oakland and Yoncalla became well known for their turkey production; in fact, Oakland once laid claim to being the "Turkey Capital of the World." Author J. V. Chenoweth explained that at one time Oakland was reported to have shipped more turkeys than any other town on the Pacific Coast. The numbers for Thanksgiving and Christmas give testament to the sheer quantity of fowl being raised in the area. In 1907, they shipped 150,000 pounds. Chenoweth also tells that turkeys were a profitable business. In 1910 alone, George Hall Jr. made a net profit of $732.35 on an initial investment of $80.00. Yoncalla had many farmers and opened a turkey-processing plant that bought birds from local farmers.

Oakland showcased an annual Northwestern Turkey Show for a week each December. In 1929, a rancher from Yoncalla walked his turkeys to Oakland in what is probably the first-ever "turkey drive." Fashioned after the cattle drives, he walked his turkeys to the Turkey Show in two days. Before beginning the trek, the birds were walked through warm tar and sand to provide a coating to protect their feet. The rancher reported that there were only a couple of casualties along the way.

The Grapevine

The Umpqua Valley's beauty is enhanced by the vineyards that line the countryside. The first vineyards of the area were planted by Adolph Doerner

Dressed turkeys ready for shipment from the J.T. Bridges warehouse in Oakland. The man seated on the truck is a turkey buyer from San Francisco. *Photo courtesy of the Douglas County Museum.*

on his farm near Melrose in 1888. When grower Tony Tringalo moved to the area in 1976, there were several commercial vineyards among the family growers. He explains, "The area has gone from cottage industries to big business. Along with selling wine, the commercial wineries have created a sub industry of weddings and banquets [on the vineyard grounds]. Local restaurants and hotels have benefitted from the winery tours." Tringalo, whose family has owned vineyards and an olive oil mill in Italy for five generations, grows a small parcel of grapes for a local winery.

The Umpqua Valley's climate is very similar to that of Napa Valley, California. The cool nights and the wide temperature changes are credited with enhancing the flavor of the grape. Modern growing methods were established in trellising to maximize the sun exposure of the fruit. Early on, most growers utilized "dry farming" in their vineyards. Today, irrigation has provided a more stable crop. Wind turbines are used in large vineyards to generate wind velocity, preventing frost damage to the plant's buds.

The wine business increased throughout Douglas County in the early 1980s. The hundred valleys of the Umpqua create dynamic growing opportunities in the area. Award-winning pinot noir and Riesling varieties have fared well in the cooler valleys, while merlot and cabernet continue to thrive in the warmer sectors. Each of the wineries offers a unique ambiance and distinct tastes for even the most discerning palate.

Prunes

In 1932, the Umpqua region was home to over ten thousand acres of prune orchards. The climate and soil were an excellent combination for the trees. Prune orchards in the county date back to about 1878, when John Hall and Jake Chadwick of Myrtle Creek planted orchards. The two most common prunes grown in the area were the Italian prune and the sweet petite prune.

In springtime, the valley was draped with the tree's white blossoms. By late summer or early fall, the bluish purple fruit of the prunes would ripen. The trees were shaken, and the dislodged prunes were then picked up off the ground. Lilly Stevenson of Canyonville recalls picking prunes as a child in 1938: "Kneepads were sewed into pants...we filled bushel baskets and carried them to a wagon. The baskets were marked to identify how many each person picked. We received three cents for a bushel of the larger Italian prunes and five cents for the smaller petite prunes. The start of the school year was sometimes delayed for picking." Prune dryers (dehydrators) were located across the county. Prunes dried for approximately eighteen to thirty-six hours before being taken to market.

Clarence Moyer owned and operated successful fruit orchards in Dillard. On a visit to the orchards in 1933, CCC worker Norman Myers described his visit to the orchard. "I ate all of the prunes I could hold in one orchard, peaches in another...Dillard is a great fruit country and also melon and berry [Alaska blackberries]. They are as big as one's thumb." In 1935, Moyer developed his own prune, the "Moyer prune," which is still quite popular today.

Douglas County's prune orchards were once valued at over $2.5 million. However, much of the market is gone today.

Workers on a prune dryer near Yoncalla. *Photo courtesy of the Douglas County Museum.*

Roll Out the Barrel

The Douglas County economy was further expanded by growing hops. This cash crop was considered "extra" income by farmers, as the harvesting was often completed by women and children. This allowed men to tend to other jobs, creating a dual income opportunity.

The hop plants produce fluffy yellow-green blooms on their vines. The plants were encouraged to climb poles up to twenty feet high. To harvest the crop, a "pole puller" was used to pry the pole and hop vines from the ground.

Vines were laid horizontally while pickers removed the blossoms. The hops were then placed in burlap bags and weighed. Pickers were paid according to weight. The next step of the process was drying the hops in a kiln dryer. For balanced drying, hops were elevated high above wood-fire furnaces, allowing the heat to circulate evenly. The dried hops were removed from the kiln to cool and then bundled in rectangular bales (similar to hay bales) for shipping.

Many of the hops were utilized by local breweries in Gardiner, Oakland and Roseburg. One pound of hops would adequately flavor one barrel of beer.

INDUSTRY

There's Gold (and Nickel) in Them Thar Hills

James Marshall discovered gold in the waters of the American River in California while building a mill for John Sutter on January 24, 1848. The discovery led to the California gold rush. The frenzied migration in California soon reached up north to Oregon as miners from around the world sought out their fortunes. Prospectors staked their claims throughout the mountains and along the streams of Douglas County. The South Umpqua territory was a hotbed for exploration. In hot and dry summer months, disputes became common between miners and farmers over water rights.

Coffee Creek Mining District

In 1852, placer digging uncovered gold at Coffee Creek located in the Texas Gulch Tributary, near Perdue (present-day Milo). This was almost seven years before Oregon became a state. Hundreds of miners and Chinese laborers quickly made their way to the valley, and soon the mining towns of Coffeeville and Tailhold were established. Miners used a variety of techniques to search for gold from the creek. One popular method was panning. The miner placed handfuls of sand and plenty of water in a pan and swirled the contents, allowing the lighter sand and particles to wash over the side, leaving the heavier gold in the pan.

Pack mules at the Coffee Creek gold mine. *Photo courtesy of the Douglas County Museum.*

Placer and hydraulic mining methods often involved the use of a wooden sluice box or a ditch called a ground sluice. The sluice is riffled to diminish the current and allow the pooling of heavier particles, where gold can settle. With hydraulic mining, the slurry (a mixture of water, rock and particles) is broken up by the use of a water cannon, which is often referred to as a "giant" by miners. In both cases, prospectors allow the mixture to flow over their sluice and then search for the gold within the tailings. It was each miner's responsibility to discard the tailings.

The gold strike was a boon to the local area as supplies were bought from the general store in Perdue. A little farther away, Canyonville and Roseburg also sold supplies to miners.

Coffee Creek is said to have gotten its name when a sick prospector continued to moan, "Oh God, I wish I had a cup of coffee!" Mining operations extended into the Depression years, often by transient miners searching for enough money to purchase a grubstake (mining essentials) and move on to mines that were then more promising.

Miles Mitchell described his experiences in the Coffee Creek mining district. He was a prospector and served as a cook for the Heller brothers who had three claims on Russell Creek. He cooked out of a nice shake cabin complete with a wood stove, bunk beds and a heater. He would give up this "golden opportunity" for the navy in World War II. Before leaving, he shoved his gold pan as far under the cabin as he could reach. In a 1993 article, Mitchell recounts coming back to the gulch twenty years later:

> *The old shake cabin was flat as a pancake, yielding to subsequent heavy snows. As I surveyed the landscape I noticed the old apple orchard still had two trees which were struggling to survive. Everything else was gone...I closed my eyes—I could hear the roar of the giant and the loud concussion of boulders crashing into each other as they cascaded down towards the sluice boxes. As I turned to leave I remembered my old gold pan, was it possible it might still be there? I clawed at a pile of rotten logs and pine shakes. Suddenly I felt the rim of the pan carefully sliding it towards me. After all those years it was still intact except for a six inch section...*[that] *rusted through.*

The China Ditch

The Myrtle Creek Consolidated Hydraulic Gold Mining and Manufacturing Company began acquiring water rights and property for mining. To accommodate the hydraulic giants, a plan was devised to run a canal from the Little River to Lee Creek. Over two hundred Chinese laborers dug a five-foot-deep ditch for some twenty-six miles reaching Tuttle Creek, which is in the North Umpqua drainage. In 1891, three crews worked around-the-clock running three giants to wash the hillsides of gold deposits. As more gold was recovered, the company's stock sales intensified. Work on the ditch continued eastward as they connected into several other streams and ran flumes over rocky terrain. Crews laid pipelines and built sluice boxes along the way. The ditch never reached the Little River, and the company failed to reach the high expectations of the project. In 1894, the company was bankrupt and sold at auction. In 1991, an eleven-mile section of the ditch was listed on the National Register of Historical Places.

Lee Creek

The Casteel Mines Company began hydraulic mining along Lee Creek in 1911. There were over fifty thousand ounces of placer gold retrieved, and the company was profitable for its stockholders. Things slowed by 1917, but in addition to gold, the miners also recovered animal tusks and shells.

Nickel Mining

The grassy meadows of Old Piney Mountain were a good place to graze sheep. One day, while tending their sheep, some herders collected a few mineral specimens. These fragments turned out to contain copper and tin and were successfully reduced to a metallic nickel. Years later, in 1882, miner Will Q. Brown moved to Riddle and launched the commercial development of the nickel. With control of over eight hundred acres for mining, Brown's crew opened shafts and tunnels removing over three thousand tons of ore. After Brown and J.B. Riddle sold off substantial acreage, the commercial interests would eventually change hands to the Hanna Company. This company joined an alliance with the federal government in 1953 to form the first major nickel mine in the United States. A tramway was built to the summit of Nickel Mountain (the new name given to Old Piney Mountain), and they added a nickel-smelting plant. The Hanna Company produced over $1 billion worth of nickel from Nickel Mountain.

The Legend of Ed Schieffelin's Gold

When Ed Schieffelin missed an appointment in town in May 1897, George Jackson headed up to his cabin to check on him. He found Schieffelin slumped over his gold pan. He had died while assaying its contents. In his diary, he had made his last entry: "Found it at last—richer than Tombstone could ever hope to be." Some of the ore nuggets were appraised at $2,000 to the ton (a unit of measure for gold). Ed's diary, however, failed to disclose one important detail: the whereabouts of his discovery.

In the 1850s, Ed and his brothers followed their father, Clinton, to the Oregon Territory in the Rogue Valley. At the age of twelve, Ed began his nomadic life as a prospector searching for gold throughout most of the West—Nevada, California and New Mexico—before he landed in Arizona. Despite warnings from army scouts, Ed decided to explore the hills along the San Pedro River. The unsettled country was home to the Apache Indians and places where leaders Geronimo and Cochise were known to frequent.

Several prospectors had been killed in this area, including Fredrick Brunckow, who had built a cabin near a small vein of silver he had discovered. Ironically, Ed used Brunckow's cabin as a shelter for his small party of men while exploring the area. They concentrated their search near the discovery of silver tailings in a dry wash. A man in the party named Lenox was killed,

Construction on the Hanna Company nickel-smelting plant, circa 1910. *Photo courtesy of the Douglas County Museum.*

and they buried him near the wash. After further exploration, Ed proved himself to be a competent prospector with the discovery of a mother lode of silver in a vein he estimated was some fifty feet long and over a foot wide. Since it was near Lenox's grave, he named his stake Tombstone when he filed his mining claim in 1877, with under a dollar left in his pocket.

Ed formed a partnership with his brother Al and Richard Gird, and by 1878, they began mining their claim. The next year would be a memorable time in the area for several reasons. Tombstone was officially established as a city. In June, Ed Schieffelin brought out his first load of silver bullion, worth $18,744 (which would equate to about $500,000 today). Later in December, Wyatt Earp and his brothers rode into town and assumed the role of lawmen. Ed and his partners would lay several more profitable claims and all become millionaires. By the mid-1880s, the town's population had boomed to about fifteen thousand people. Ed's brother Al built the Schieffelin Hall as a theater, which still remains in Tombstone.

The partners eventually sold out their stakes and moved on. In 1882, Ed married Mary Brown and built a large home near Alameda, California, as he prepared to settle down. But those wanderlust tendencies soon returned, along with the lure of prospecting for gold. For years, he followed the gold strikes across the West until coming full circle back to visit his brothers Eff and Jay in southern Oregon. He loaded up his gear and team of horses and made his way through Canyonville to begin panning for gold in the creeks and rivers around the abandoned Coffee Creek mines.

He left behind the easy, more modern life of the city for an old prospector's cabin near Days Creek. Ed kept a diary, often scratching down notes while hiking through the wilderness. He was a strong hiker who could cover a lot of terrain on his trips. After prospecting on an overnight trip in and out of rain, Schieffelin hadn't lost his touch after all those years. He had landed on a site more promising in his estimation than the legendary mother lode of silver in Tombstone. He triumphantly returned to his cabin to more closely examine his loot. However, he died before he finished assaying the value.

So many questions remain today. Where did he find that gold? How far away had he wandered? Where was Ed Schieffelin's last discovery? Some of the finest prospectors have made it a life-long ambition to find Ed's gold, crisscrossing over miles of rugged territory. Despite all their efforts, no one is known to have found the place. To this day, the location of Ed Schieffelin's discovery is still a mystery, and a mother lode of gold remains hidden somewhere in them thar hills.

FORESTRY AND TIMBER

Since its inception, the timber industry has played a vital role in the economy of Douglas County. This industry has seen many changes over the years attributed to several key factors. The advancement of technology has streamlined the ability to economically and safely remove timber from remote areas. In some cases, this has caused over extraction of forestlands and has led to the endangerment of other natural resources in this fragile environment.

The timber industry developed in the Lower Umpqua Estuaries. With an abundance of timber close to the river, loggers felled trees and rafted them down to the Gardiner sawmill. Here they were loaded onto ships bound for San Francisco. Sawmills quickly began appearing throughout the county. John Kellogg started his mill in Kellogg in 1849. Other notable mills included Moses Dyer's water-powered mill near Myrtle Creek, Franklin Sutherlin's mill on Calapooia Creek and a slash-type mill near Drain on Pass Creek.

Along with the mills came logging camps. The life of a lumberjack was tough, and the days were long. The timber companies often provided bunkhouses and a cook tent for the loggers, who were paid by the hour and then charged for room and board. The three square meals were provided by the cook. The cook's job was considered by most companies to be one of the most important. It was said that the camp that provided the best food got the best workers.

Depending on the location of the timber harvest, some workers lived in town and shared a vehicle, referred to as the "crummy," to the work site. Bud Schosso moved his family several times to towns near camps. His daughter Gertrude remembers, "My dad worked long hours. When they left in the morning it was still dark, and they returned in the crummy after dark. If the logging camp was too far off, Dad would stay there and come home on weekends."

In addition to the company logger, there were independent loggers known as "gyppos." Some gyppos had contracts for their lumber while others logged trees, uncertain if there was a paycheck for their labor. Author William Robbins described a gyppo logger as a "hardy individual who worked on marginal capital, usually through subcontracts with a major company or broker, and whose equipment was invariably pieced together with baling wire."

In the early years, the Gardiner Mill Company, which continually upgraded its equipment, dominated the lumber industry in Douglas County.

Timber fallers with a Douglas fir tree twenty-eight feet in circumference. Two men are on springboards, while the third man is lying in the kerf. *Photo courtesy of the Douglas County Museum.*

In 1904, a visit from a columnist for the *Timberman* toured the facility, noting that it was a "splendid mill" utilizing modern technology.

The introduction of a mechanical pulley system, called "the donkey," to the logging industry had an immediate impact on productivity. The donkey, equipped with a small engine, pulled logs up to the landings with rope or cable. The machine replaced the widely used animals—donkeys and oxen. It was also used on ships for loading timber. The arrival of the railroad was beneficial in getting lumber to market in a timely manner.

Early on, cedars were used for boatbuilding, while spruce was a preferred lumber for airplanes. In the post–World War II housing boom, the Douglas fir became popular, and Roseburg would become a dominant player. The city was on the main railroad line and nestled within some of the world's finest timber.

The Douglas County Lumber Company was established outside of Glide on Rock Creek in 1941. The original sawmill secured its own timber from both private and federal lands. The company, under the leadership of Sid Comfort and Maurice Hallmark, had about one hundred employees living in company housing. They expanded onto an additional ten acres, located in Roseburg. However, the residents of Roseburg complained of the dust and soot released from the wigwam burners. The company is now Douglas County Forest Products and is located outside Winchester.

Kenneth Ford successfully turned a small sawmill into the Roseburg Forest Products Company, which is the largest family-held lumber products company in the world. The company has expanded its base of Oregon mills to facilities across the United States, now offering the broadest product line in the country. The Ford Family Foundation was established in 1996 and is one of the largest charitable foundations in Oregon.

While timber is a highly sought-after commodity, trees and forests are vital to the survival of salmon, birds and many other animal and plant species. They provide oxygen and create a natural canopy to aid in the moderation of temperatures. In 1905, the National Forest Service was carved out of the Division of Forestry. Their forest service roads and firefighters protect timberlands. The law enforcement division closely monitors activities in the forest, including the timber industry. Scientists, along with the Fish and Game Department, weigh the impact of logging on wildlife habitats.

As early as 1907, President Theodore Roosevelt enlarged the Cascade Range Forest Reserve to temper relationships between conservationists and loggers. Bureau of Land Management lands have been created for public use and conservation of valuable acreage. This continues to be a challenging environment today. Efforts to protect wildlife like the spotted owl and the streams for salmon have accounted for lost jobs and diminished timber receipts. Timber dollars have historically funded libraries, law enforcement and even veteran services. There is an ongoing effort to create a balance between continued protections and sustainable timber harvest on previously logged acreage.

FISHING

In addition to catching fish as a staple of their diet, natives can be attributed with establishing the foundations for commercial fishing in Douglas County. There is record as early as 1791 of Lower Umpqua Indians trading salmon for goods with passing ships. Early explorers David Douglas and Reverend Gustavus Hines also noticed a Native American fishery near Sawyers Rapids that produced a large supply of both salmon and trout. In August 1840, Hines described the fishery in his journal: "The river rushes over a ledge of rocks in a number of narrow channels, and falling about twenty-five feet in so many rods, forms a fine salmon fishery."

William Rose was one of the region's first commercial fishermen. He operated a fishery near the convergence of the North and South Umpqua Rivers. In 1874, he utilized the railroad to ship fresh trout and salmon as far as Portland. On August 17, 1874, the *Plaindealer* wrote of his enterprise:

> *William Rose, who owns the fishery at Umpqua Junction (the Forks) is supplying the market and the surrounding county with the finest fish ever taken from any water. Speckled trout, salmon trout and salmon of every size are taken by him in sufficient quantity to supply all who apply to purchase. Persons along the line of the railroad can be supplied by sending their orders to Mr. Rose. Fish caught in the evening at the Umpqua fishery can be taken to Albany, Salem and Portland by the next evening, fresh as when they were caught in the river.*

A few years later, former riverboat captain Alfred Reed developed the Gardiner-area salmon canneries on what would become Cannery Island. The island, which was located just across the river from Gardiner, had gross sales of $120,000 in 1877. Much of the work in the canneries was provided by Chinese laborers.

The Hume brothers, who owned a cannery along the Columbia River in Washington State, began to send Chinese crews to the Umpqua River as well. In 1871, they processed over seven hundred cans of salmon. Between 1923 and 1946, the fishing industry contributed handsomely to the area's economy when over twenty million pounds of salmon were processed. But soon, the commercial industry declined due to overfishing. Also, in 1910, the Oregon Fish Commission began a five-year program where they harvested an estimated twenty-four million Chinook salmon eggs for hatcheries on other Oregon rivers. This resulted in smaller salmon runs.

Currently, most of the fishing on the Umpqua River is done for recreation. The region offers world-class fly-fishing on its rivers. Along with salmon and trout, sturgeon and bass are plentiful. In fact, during the flood of 1964, the waters overflowed the fish hatchery troughs in Reedsport, allowing thousands of small-mouth bass to be introduced into the Umpqua River. As a result, small-mouth bass have become much more abundant on the Umpqua River. The state and county have established strict regulations on salmon and trout fishing, enabling the fish to make a comeback from the days of overuse.

7

Presidential Shortcomings

Few things stir up enthusiasm like a presidential visit. A sense of pride and patriotic spirit fills the air as crowds anxiously await a glimpse of America's commander in chief. In 1880, President Rutherford B. Hayes made a trip through Douglas County. He was the first sitting president to visit the county.

On September 25, 1880, the Hayes entourage rode the California & Oregon Railroad to Redding, California, which was the terminus of the track heading north. After spending the night, the Hayes party boarded a stagecoach and headed north. By the morning of Monday the twenty-seventh, the party had departed Yreka and set out for Oregon across the rugged Siskiyou Mountains. Interestingly, the notorious Black Bart had passed over this same remote route just a few days earlier. Near the summit of Siskiyou Pass, Bart had successfully robbed a stagecoach.

After lodging in Jacksonville and then the Wolf Creek Inn, President Hayes made his way down Sexton Pass and into Canyonville. The Concord stage arrived in town pulled by a team of six matching gray horses, to the delight of area schoolchildren, who were let out of classes to greet the president. General Sherman, who rode with the group, was cheered by the local Civil War veterans. The entourage was treated to lunch at the Overland Hotel on Mrs. Wollenberg's fine china before making their way to Myrtle Creek, where Hayes had a short layover and spoke to schoolchildren there.

The president arrived in Roseburg to a cheering crowd. After General Joseph Lane greeted Hayes, the president told the enthusiastic crowd that

Rutherford B. Hayes, nineteenth president of the United States, visited Douglas County in 1880. *Photo courtesy of the Douglas County Museum.*

he had made the trip not to give speeches but because he wanted to see Oregon and meet its people. While in Roseburg, President Hayes and his wife were dinner guests at the Willis home, where they spent the night. Following dinner, there was a reception at the Metropolitan Hotel. Early the next morning, they boarded the train and had breakfast at the Thomas Hotel in Oakland before heading off for Portland. Their short visit to the county made for an exciting couple of days.

Theodore Roosevelt's trip to Oregon in 1903 was not nearly as captivating. In Grants Pass, a large crowd, including not one but two bands, anxiously waited as the train approached. However, they stood there silently as the train rolled past. Evidently, the train's engineer had forgotten to stop. Things didn't get any more exciting in Roseburg, where the president stopped for an entire five minutes. It was 2:30 a.m., and Roosevelt was sound asleep in his Pullman car. His visit did make the headlines of Roseburg's newspaper, the *Plaindealer.*

James Inman of Lookingglass nominated himself as a presidential candidate in 1904. He ran as an Independent with a socialist platform of fourteen principles. One principle was a vow not to make speeches, which made it hard, if not impossible, for him to get his message out to the entire country, especially in 1904.

The *Plaindealer* did mentioned Inman on August 25, 1904:

> *There is at last arisen one man in Oregon who is willing to get out and assert his rights by declaring himself independent candidate for President. He not only declares he is in the race but he will have a platform far superior to anything of the kind that has ever been written, and in fact is way ahead of the times...*

He was ahead of his time on several issues, including his selection of a female running mate. Maybe he was too far ahead, as she was unable to contribute her vote to the ticket. A fourteen-thousand-word account outlining his platform for the *Roseburg Review* in October 1904 failed to make it to press as he was waiting for his accompanying photograph to be processed.

The paper's editor wrote that since Inman had neglected to get his name officially placed on any ballots, it was unlikely that, with only five weeks until the election, he would have any chance as an Independent against the other candidates. In the end, Inman could lay claim to receiving at least one write-in vote in the 1904 presidential election. In good taste, he did send a congratulatory letter to Theodore Roosevelt on his victory.

8

Cops and Robbers

There has long been a criminal element that permeates the seemingly tightknit fabric of society. From its inception, Douglas County lawmen and investigators have diligently strived to match wits with criminals who have sought to undermine the law in search of easy money and, often, fame.

STAGED HEIST

On the night of June 13, 1879, a stage was loaded in Roseburg for delivery on the Oregon Stage Company's Roseburg–Redding, California route. Well-respected driver Dan Smith stored the miscellaneous baggage in the rear boot of the coach. He then placed the more valuable registered mail pouches in the express box, which was kept near the driver in the front boot. The wooden express boxes were about twenty inches long, a foot wide and about ten inches high. To protect the valuable contents, the boxes were fortified with iron straps.

The stage made numerous stops along the route, where the horses were fed or the teams were exchanged to keep them fresh for the long journey. At their scheduled stop in Myrtle Creek, a routine check of the freight revealed a startling discovery. One of the registered mail pouches was missing.

Postal investigators quickly arrived on the scene. Despite performing a thorough search of the entire route, there was no sign of the bag. Smith believed there must have been a mistake as he had two passengers on the seat beside him on the entire trip. He insisted it was impossible for someone to have stolen the bags, and it was improbable they were lost in transit. The authorities continued to investigate, but the pouch, which contained $4,800 in gold dust, had all but disappeared.

As the investigation seemed to be winding down, Dan Smith continued driving for the stage, and there was no unusual activity involving his finances. In August, his wife and two children moved in with her ailing parents in Shasta, California. While they were gone, Smith became smitten with a married woman, and the two were said to have left the country together.

The postal service hired local man John Fullerton, who had ties to all the parties involved with the stage that night, to continue the investigation. A man named Riley, who was a hostler at the Oak Grove station (a stop before Myrtle Creek), was questioned by Fullerton and kept under close surveillance. He was making frequent visits to a girl near Canyonville. Fullerton, feeling that he must have some knowledge of the robbery, hired the girl's neighbor as an informant. Fullerton's instincts were correct, as the informant learned that the girl and Riley were getting married. Riley's girlfriend had also mentioned that Riley had recently found a lode of gold in a gulch near Oak Grove and, as she put it, "had plenty of money."

Fullerton confronted Riley and struck a deal with him that if he told everything he knew of that night, he might avoid punishment. Riley complied, telling that he and Smith had worked together on the heist. At the Oak Grove stop, Riley selected the heaviest pouch and cut it open, removing the gold dust. He filled the bag with rocks and threw it into the South Umpqua River. He took Fullerton to the exact spot, and they recovered the bag that same afternoon. Fullerton questioned the man who sat on the coach seat next to Smith that night with his wife. (It was his wife with whom Smith had run off.) He admitted to witnessing the entire theft just as Riley had accounted. He maintained his innocence and didn't know the whereabouts of the two. The man was acquitted of any wrongdoing.

Fullerton traveled to Shasta, California, and located Mrs. Dan Smith. Upon informing her that Smith was a suspect in the crime and that he was involved with another woman, she began to talk. The name Dan Smith was an alias for Andrew Humason. Mrs. Smith then led Fullerton to his mother in Waloa, Texas.

In September, Fullerton headed to Texas. He disguised himself as a farmer interested in buying land. He grew a beard and masterfully befriended Dan's mother, who informed him that Dan and his new wife were in Seymour, Texas, to buy land. Fullerton would arrest him in a local restaurant. He was brought back to Oregon and given a seven-year sentence in the state penitentiary.

BLACK BART

The Roseburg–Redding and Roseburg–Yreka Stages became frequent targets for Black Bart. Over eight years, he is credited with at least twenty-eight successful holdups. His escapades as a "road agent," a term used for stagecoach robbers, began in California. Bart stood out by being polite and actually saying please when he asked for the mail pouches and the express box. He was nicknamed "The Poet," as he often left behind notes like this one: "I've labored long for bread, for honor and for riches, but on my corns too long you've tread. You fine haired sons of bitches. Black Bart, the Po8."

He wore work clothes and a linen duster with a flour sack over his head. Armed with a twelve-gauge shotgun, he usually approached stages that were slowed while climbing hills. He also preferred nights when the moon was bright. After success in California, he eventually crossed the border to try his luck in Oregon in September 1880. After several more successful holdups, Bart returned to California.

The Roseburg Stage continued to be his primary target. Finally, on November 3, 1883, as Bart was fleeing the scene under a barrage of bullets, he dropped a key piece of evidence. Wells Fargo detective James Hume found a handkerchief with an identifying laundry mark. This led them to Charles Boles, who was living under the alias of Charles Bolton in San Francisco, California. Investigators were surprised to hear that he never carried bullets for his gun, as he didn't want to hurt anyone. Bart pleaded guilty to only his last robbery and served four years in San Quentin. After his release, he disappeared from the public's eye. However, for years afterward, rumors tied him to stage robberies throughout the West.

The Great Oregon Train Robbery

The superstitious would marvel at the coincidence on October 11, 1923, as Train No. 13, known as the Gold Special, headed up the steep 4 percent grade toward Tunnel 13 with the aid of a helper engine. Before reaching Tunnel 13, the train made its scheduled stop at the Siskiyou Station. Here, the additional engine was uncoupled as the crew checked the airbrakes for the steep descent down the other side.

The train had originated from Portland, making its way south without incident, stopping at the railroad division point of Roseburg to pick up mailbags and passengers. Three brothers—Roy, Ray and Hugh DeAutremont—believed there was $40,000 in cash onboard the Railway Post Office in the mail car. They waited patiently near the tunnel that day, intending to ambush the train.

Twin brothers Ray and Roy had been drifters who were in and out of jobs. While living in an apartment in Salem, they considered robbing area banks and businesses to obtain some easy money. Their sights, however, turned to the train in the winter of 1922, when Ray rode the train south from Salem to visit his brother Hugh in New Mexico. Upon graduating high school, Hugh would join them in the heist.

After carefully scouting the entire Portland–San Francisco route, they decided on Tunnel 13, as the train would be moving slowly enough for them to board. Figuring the mail car would be locked, they stole explosives and a detonator from a construction site. Loaded with camping gear and provisions, the brothers hiked up and canvassed the area around the tunnel. Their plan for the robbery and escape was meticulous. Roy and Hugh waited near the entrance at the east side of the 3,100-foot-long tunnel. Ray waited with his shotgun at the west end. The explosives and detonator were laid alongside the tracks.

As the train crept into the tunnel, Roy and Hugh jumped aboard. Hugh ordered engineer Sidney Bates to stop the train as he held him and fireman Marvin Seng at bay with his pistol. Ray, who quickly boarded the train, fired at the mail clerk, Elvyn Dougherty, who was locking the car door. With the train stopped, the heist was going as planned. They applied the explosives to the door of the mail car and set them off, not realizing there was far too much dynamite. They completely destroyed the car, killing Dougherty.

Confusion set in as the tunnel quickly filled with smoke. As their plan unraveled, the unnerved brothers would shoot and kill the engineer, a fireman and a brakeman before fleeing the scene. Wanted posters and rewards were posted around the world. It wasn't until four years later, in 1927, that the brothers were caught. All three had invented aliases. Hugh had joined the army and was apprehended in the Philippines. Ray and Roy were taken into custody in Steubenville, Ohio. Ironically, the mail car had only contained mail parcels.

The Cold Case Squad

Coupled by a tight budget and a shortage of man hours at the Sheriff's Department, the cold case files in Douglas County were increasingly mounting, being set aside for more pressing issues. In 2002, in an attempt to lighten the workload, Jim Main placed an ad asking for the help of volunteers. After weeding out the numerous candidates through interviews and background checks, an elite group of four retired lawmen were chosen to head the nation's first-ever all-volunteer Cold Case Squad.

Armed with years of investigative experience, the savvy group of Syd Boyle, Tom Hall, Al Olsen and Thomas Schultz were sworn in as officers. A breath of new life was given to the old, unsolved homicide cases as the squad blew the dust off the cold case files and began investigating.

"We didn't know each other coming into the squad," Syd explains of the multi-skilled squad members. Syd began his career in law enforcement in 1962 at age twenty-one, working for the Watsonville, California police department. He is a fingerprint expert, and his photography skills had come in handy for crime scene investigations. Syd has investigated over one hundred homicides.

After receiving a degree in criminal justice, Tom Hall worked as a U.S. postal inspector. Specializing in mail bombs, he also investigated homicides, robberies and burglaries. Later, as a postal facility security specialist, his emphasis was on postal and identity theft.

Thomas Schultz was happy to volunteer time to the squad to give back to the community. During his career, he had served as a police detective in Wisconsin and California, along with a stint in Las Vegas.

With a degree in public administration, Al Olsen served as a detective and lieutenant commander of an investigation division before later becoming a police chief in Morro Bay and Pacifica, California. His career spans thirty years.

"We each read the case files (which can contain several binders of information) separately. If we read them together, it could become convoluted," Syd explains. Often after reviewing the cases, one or more of them chime in with, "I had a case just like that once." With their vast experience in fighting crime, they have also resorted to a few old tricks to obtain information. In one case, they put a snitch into the cell with a suspect.

Syd also points out that some squad members have traveled as far as Florida and Arizona to interview persons of interest. "Many don't realize that people move over time. And some people might be willing to tell more than they did at the time of the initial investigation. Old girlfriends are now ex-girlfriends and such."

Their first case was the murder of Benny Lee King. For twenty-eight years this case had gone unsolved. In January 2003, the Cold Case Squad was assigned the case. By May, they had the case solved with a conviction.

At a press conference following that trial, the four dressed in casual attire, including three of them wearing cowboy hats. As they entertained questions from the press, a reference was made to them as the "Cold Case Cowboys," referring to the movie *Space Cowboys*. The name stuck, although the Douglas County Sheriff's Office prefers their official title of Cold Case Squad.

The detectives appeared on *Dateline* with Stone Phillips and have been featured in numerous newspapers and magazines around the world. Their first case was the topic of *Cold Case Files* Episode 69, which aired on A&E. Although their lineup has been shuffled over the years, the Cold Case Squad continues to investigate cases, solving and updating unsolved mysteries in Douglas County.

9

And Along Came Uncle Sam

The Army's Fort Umpqua

Indian agent Joel Palmer began the roundup of Native Americans from 1853 to 1856 for relocation to the Siletz Reservation. To contain the two thousand Indians within the 125-mile-long reservation, Fort Yamhill, Fort Hoskins and the Siletz Blockhouse were built to solidify the north and east boundaries. In 1856, the army's Fort Umpqua was established as a southern fortress near Winchester Bay and Umpqua City.

With the rise of Scottsburg as a bustling shipping port, Umpqua City's fortunes were waning. The once-bustling city had been reduced to a post office and a few buildings owned by Indian agent Edward Drew, who rented several to the government for the army's fort.

Captain Joseph Stewart was the first commanding officer. There were eighty-three men on his roster. The fort was built in an isolated area surrounded by sand dunes, and soon it was dubbed "The Lonely Outpost." Life at the fort was considered dull. Low morale and desertions quickly became a problem. Adding to the misery of the soldiers was the dreary weather. A physician on the base, Dr. Edward Vollum, began recording the region's weather patterns. The Lonely Outpost laid claim to the wettest military outpost in the United States, with over seventy inches of annual rainfall.

The Siletz Reservation had remained peaceful over the years, and in July 1862, instructions were issued from the Department of Pacific Headquarters that "Fort Umpqua will be abandoned forthwith." The deserted land and buildings were transferred to the Siuslaw National Forest by President Hoover in 1931.

THE CIVILIAN CONSERVATION CORPS

I propose to create a civilian conservation corps to be used in simple work, not interfering with normal employment, and confining itself to forestry, the prevention of soil erosion, flood control and similar projects. I call your attention to the fact that this type of work is of definite, practical value, not only through the prevention of great present financial loss, but also as a means of creating future national wealth.
—Franklin D. Roosevelt

In 1933, President Roosevelt began what was considered a profusion of executive orders by implementing programs of the New Deal. This series of economic programs was designed for young men who were having difficulty finding employment during the Great Depression. The Civilian Conservation Corps was the most popular of these national work relief programs. It created a core of unskilled manual labor jobs for the development and conservation of our natural resources. The corps provided room, board and clothing, and it paid a small wage. Workers were expected to send most of their earnings home to their families. Douglas MacArthur placed U.S. Army reserve officers in charge of the individual camps. The CCC camps began to spring up in Douglas County in 1933.

Camp Devil's Flat F-36 was built east of Azalea and was under the command of navy commander Lieutenant L.S. Tishnor. Men were given a physical at local armories and assigned to the camp. LEM (local experienced men) who had experience in forestry, logging or road-building were hired to train the "junior" or rookie recruits. The company was dubbed "The Fire Eaters" for their service as firefighters; this company of men also excelled in building roads.

In 1935, the outfit was renumbered as Company 2904 and assigned Camp Number F-117. An advance group of men from the camp was sent out to establish Camp South Umpqua Falls near Tiller, Oregon. This group set up about thirty army teepee-style tents in what was originally intended to be a

The CCC Company 1305 of Azalea in 1934. The company later moved and built U.S. Forest Service buildings in Tiller. *Photo courtesy of the Douglas County Museum.*

"summer" camp. However, later the CCC would abandon these temporary shelters for permanent barracks. Eventually, the 2904 closed shop in Azalea and moved into the new camp, which included amenities such as showers and flush toilets, water heaters and even a laundry facility.

In addition to building roads, they built a ranger residence and other dwellings in the historic Tiller Ranger Station. Company 2904 also constructed fire lookouts, shelters and guard stations throughout the area. The Ranger Station is still in use today, including a historical residence, complete with photos, newspapers and other artifacts from over the years.

Norman Myers from Nebraska worked in several Douglas County CCC camps. In his letters home, he gives a rare firsthand account of what life was like in the camps during the Depression. Here is an excerpt from a letter written on February 18, 1934, in Camas Valley, Oregon:

Dear Folks:
It is Sunday evening...I worked at the gravel pit again last Friday. They got red dynamite in now. They have more kinds of dynamite than I ever dreamed of. We sure have a high ledge now. They don't have [reliable] brakes on the trucks and one stopped near the pit. Another behind it couldn't stop so is wrecked quite a bit...I came to the main camp on Friday evening. I always get sick riding in the back end of the truck on the rough roads. The Rotary Club of Roseburg gave a splendid program in the recreation hall in the evening. One thing that is true is that the Oregonian people are hospitable. They had a local magician who was

Civilian Conservation Corps Camp Tyee. *Photo courtesy of the Douglas County Museum.*

exceedingly clever. He sure pulled some fast ones on some of the kids. They brought some fine singers.

They have announced that the time for signing up again is next Thursday. Unless the next letter [from his parents] *says differently I am going to sign to go back. One hardly knows what to do. If I sign up again I would have to stay a year and then I would have the same problem again. Of course, a job is a job and I would hate to be out of work anymore. However, I would like to try to get a job in private industry if possible. If one does not sign again, he can never get in the CCC's again. Only four Fremont* [Nebraska] *men are in the camp now. Only one thinks that he might stay...I know I can at least exist and if I can't get a job I can husk corn next fall...I have earned quite a bit out of this so far, about $200.00 I suppose. There is no chance of finding a job out here without pull or a lot of luck.*

In the uncertain times during the Great Depression, many men like Norman Myers would continue to re-sign with the corps to guarantee work and a dependable paycheck. The program built many roads and parks throughout the county. The enrollees were often referred to as the "Tree Army" and are credited with planting over two million trees. With the demands of the World War II efforts, funding for the Civilian Conservation Corp was ended by Congress in 1942.

THE JUNGLEERS

World War II veteran James Marr of Roseburg survives as the lone sentinel from the Douglas County contingent of the 41st Infantry Division. Marr's introduction to the military was through the National Guard. His outfit was known as the 162nd Infantry, Company D, 1st Battalion, of the 41st Division. In early 1942, the group was summoned to Fort Lewis, Washington, and boarded a train east to Fort Dix, New Jersey. From there, the troops were transported to the Brooklyn Naval Yard, where they boarded a ship for a forty-five-day trip.

The entire time, the soldiers had no idea where they were being commissioned. The ship looped south, passing through the Panama Canal and finally arriving in Australia in April 1942. Here they received more training alongside Australian troops. The division then headed to New Guinea to battle the Japanese forces, becoming the first combat division to go on the offensive in the South Pacific.

The division received a commendation for spending an unprecedented seventy-six consecutive days in contact with enemy forces without rest or relief. Their meager supplies were dropped out of airplanes, and the soldiers had to share rations, going days at a time on half rations. "Everyone was looking out for the other guy, not looking out for our own safety, but for those around us," said Marr.

James Marr of the 41st Infantry Division. His division was dubbed the "Jungleers" for their efforts against the Japanese in the islands of the South Pacific during World War II. *Photo courtesy of James Marr.*

117

James would be forced to leave the theater of operations when he contracted dengue fever. He explains, "I could not even keep water down. They thought I would die before they could get me to a hospital." In his condition, a long flight back home was ruled out, so James recuperated in the South Pacific for several months before returning home to Roseburg.

The 41ˢᵗ Division continued its campaign to push back the Japanese while disrupting their operations. Many of the forces succumbed to yellow fever, malaria and dengue fever during this campaign. The division was dubbed "The Jungleers" as it flushed the enemy out of the island jungles of the South Pacific while working its way toward the Philippines.

Among the medals and memorabilia that James Marr proudly displays is the Sunset Patch the division men wore on their sleeves. This gave them another distinction as the "Sunset Division." After the war, U.S. Highway 26 out of Portland officially became known as the Sunset Highway. It is named in the division's honor.

THE BUTLER BUTTE LOOKOUT

After the Japanese attack on Pearl Harbor on December 7, 1941, the War Department worked in cooperation with the U.S. Forest Service to use the Butler Butte Lookout, located in the southeastern portion of the county, as an Aircraft Warning System. Clarence and Laura Hartley worked with the Fourth Fighter Command of the U.S. Army Air Force to watch for enemy aircraft. The Japanese military also launched balloon bombs full of deadly hydrogen. Each balloon carried five bombs—four were incendiaries, and the fifth was a high-explosive antipersonnel bomb. With night-and-day operations, the Hartleys were in constant communications with the Tiller Ranger Station, connected with a ground circuit telephone line. There was also a "filter command center" located in Roseburg. Tiller Ranger Station documents explain that "because of Butler Butte's excellent radio reception, it was used to help relay weather information between various military airfields." There were no visitors allowed in the lookout as it contained a secret codebook. The Butte's code identification number was HOW76. After the war, the lookout continued to be used during the fire seasons.

10

Triumphs and Tragedies

THE DRAIN BLACK SOX

Timber Mill owner Harold Woolley brought more than jobs to the community
of Drain. In 1952, he began sponsoring an amateur baseball team called
the Drain Black Sox. Local amateur and semipro teams were very popular
during this time as there was not as much access to the professional baseball
games as there is today. Harold and his wife, Donna, loved baseball and
went to great lengths to fund a winning team. In addition to building a nice
ballpark, they bought the finest equipment as well. The roster was made up
of mostly college players. Players were paid wages to work for the Woolley
Logging Company, but they spent most of their time playing baseball
(although this was in violation of the NCAA's policies). The team was lodged
at the El Camino Motel.

In 1958, the team had a banner year, with a record of 54-4, and it earned
a spot in the field of thirty-one teams at the National Baseball Congress
Tournament in Wichita, Kansas. The National Baseball Congress, comprising
fifteen semipro and amateur leagues, was founded in 1934. The tournament,
featuring the best teams from around the country, was known as the NBC
World Series. Many NBC players went on to succeed in the professional ranks
of Major League Baseball. Since 1975, the NBC has recognized a "Graduate
of the Year" after each tournament. Past winners include Major League
Baseball All Stars Albert Pujols, Tony Gwynn and Dave Winfield.

Drain Black Sox team photo, circa 1950s. The 1958 team won the National NBC championship. *Photo courtesy of the Douglas County Museum.*

In 1958, Coach Ray Stratton and the team played a grueling schedule throughout Canada, Idaho and Washington, with many back-to-back games. To accommodate the team's travels, Woolley bought three station wagons for transportation.

The team won the Oregon State Tourney, which qualified it for the national tourney in mid-August. In a highly competitive group of teams, the San Diego Marines were touted as heavy favorites to win it all. The odds makers gave the Drain Black Sox little (if any) chance of advancing far in the tournament. The characteristics that stood out with this scrappy Black Sox squad, however, were the players' tenacity and resolve to win.

They displayed their grit during their first game on Lawrence Field with a come-from-behind win in the bottom of the ninth inning, winning 5–4 over Macon, Georgia. After a second win against Milwaukee, the Black Sox were paired against the tourney favorite, San Diego. A stunned crowd watched under the lights as the Black Sox gave it their all and whipped the Marines 10–5.

After three more wins, the Black Sox record stood at 6-0. It all came down to a rematch with the Alpine, Texas Cowboys for the tournament championship. (The Drain squad had recently startled the Cowboys with a come-from-behind victory in the ninth inning.) In the finale, as they took a 5–2 lead into the final inning, the Cowboys could smell victory. However, the relentless Black Sox scored six runs and held off the Cowboys for an 8–7 victory.

The Black Sox had defied the odds, and the team from the small logging town of Drain became National Champions by winning the NBC World Series.

THE HUNDRED-YEAR FLOODS

By the mid-1800s, Umpqua and Douglas Counties had diligently continued to expand their infrastructures. Scottsburg's economy was in an upswing as settlers and shipments continued to arrive from San Francisco. As the main city in Umpqua County, Scottsburg was also the hub of the newly completed Military Wagon Road to Myrtle Creek, which provided access to inland markets.

Then, along came a natural disaster in 1861 that would decimate the region, changing the landscape forever. Beginning in November, storms carried substantial rainfall to the region. This, coupled with melting snow, caused the Umpqua River to overflow its banks. The swift-moving current of the swollen river raised havoc on everything in its path.

The initial crest of the raging waters washed away warehouses and stores in both Upper and Lower Scottsburg, causing the loss of thirty tons of goods. The torrential rains continued, and a second crest washed away Levi Scott's sawmill along with the entire Lower Scottsburg town site. Cattle and livestock drowned as entire barns and buildings were carried away in the strong current. The flood crested at Roseburgh and Winchester the night of December 8. Water stood six feet deep at the mouth of Deer Creek. The flour mill reportedly lost over eight thousand bushels of grain. The Moore Brothers' newly constructed covered bridge at Winchester floated away. The flood was considered the worst the natives had ever seen.

Just over one hundred years later, the Christmas Day flood of 1964 was a large-scale, statewide flood that caused over $150 million in damages. Twenty people lost their lives. Several areas in central Oregon received up to two-thirds of their annual rainfall in a matter of one week.

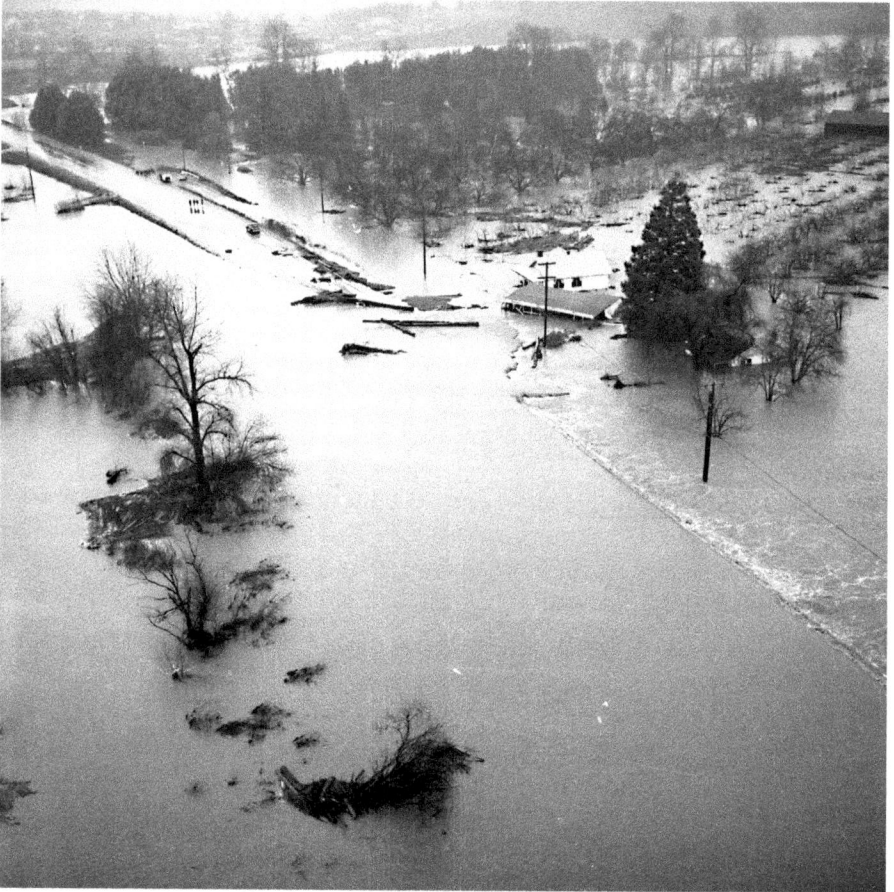

The South Umpqua River flooded a house and fruit stand in Winston during the 1964 Christmas flood. *Photo courtesy of the Douglas County Museum.*

Reedsport, which had long been susceptible to flooding, recorded over twenty-two inches of rain—almost double their normal amount for the month of December. The city has since constructed a dike system to protect the lower-lying areas of town. The dikes are frequently used to control floodwaters. They can be opened and closed as needed to channel the water away from the city.

The Roseburg Blast: A Survivor's Journey

The eerie scene was almost surreal on that fateful morning of August 7, 1959. The summer sun's rays struggled to penetrate the haze that clouded the Roseburg sky. A stench from smoldering rubble wafted throughout the city as random fires burned the ravaged buildings and vehicles. Twisted metal beams towered uselessly over dismantled piles of concrete and brick walls, resembling a war zone. There were almost unimaginable reports of damage and countless missing persons and deaths caused by an explosion.

However, statistics do not tell the entire story of the blast. What remains beyond the statistics, beyond the broken glass and piles of rubble, is the utter devastation of families whose lives were shattered within seconds. These families not only lost their earthly possessions but also suffered the grief and incomprehensible loss of their loved ones.

Earlier, in June 1959, Sabra Unrath graduated from Roseburg High School, followed soon by her birthday on July 5. Her father, Bill, bought her a special necklace that matched a favorite ring she had purchased earlier. After enrolling in Southern Oregon University for the fall semester, she headed off to Tyee, Oregon, to work as a Campfire Girls counselor, teaching archery. Everything seemed to be going as planned, and her life "was good."

Meanwhile, on August 6, 1959, George Rutherford drove his Ford truck into downtown Roseburg for a scheduled delivery to the Garretsen's Building and Supply Company. He arrived about 8:30 p.m. on the hot summer evening of a day on which the temperature had neared the century mark. An employee instructed him to park his truck near the corner of Pine and Oak Streets, and they would unload it in the morning. Rutherford walked three blocks up Oak Street for dinner and lodging at the Umpqua Hotel. About 10:00 p.m., he walked down to check that all was well with his truck before turning in for the night.

He awoke to the sound of blaring sirens as emergency vehicles made their way to a fire that had started in or near the Garretsen's warehouse. The warehouse held flammable paints, thinners, wood and gasoline. Passerby Dennis Tandy stopped his car and attempted to put out a fire burning in a row of trashcans in front of the warehouse, while his wife drove to a nearby service station to call the fire department. The flames were intense as the fire raged. At 1:07 a.m., a fire truck arrived on the scene, and the crew was hosing down the flames using a nearby hydrant.

The Roseburg 1959 blast damage. This view is looking west on Oak Street near the epicenter of the blast. *Photo courtesy of the Douglas County Museum.*

The sirens also awoke the Unrath family, who lived directly across the street, next to their Coca-Cola Bottling Company. Bill, a trained volunteer firefighter, immediately went to the roof of his own building to attach hoses and sprinklers in an attempt to prevent the roof from catching fire. Sabra's mother, Eleanor, watched the fire from the corner of the block. She witnessed panic-stricken Rutherford running down Oak Street yelling, "I have to move my truck!" It was too late when firefighters saw the ghostly EXPLOSIVES sign on Rutherford's truck. At 1:14 a.m., the flames ignited the truck, which was loaded with two tons of dynamite and over four tons of a powerful blasting agent known as ammonium nitrate.

Later that morning, Sabra received the news that there had been a fire, and she was driven back to Roseburg. Her request to listen for information on the car radio was denied. She was taken to her grandparents' home a few miles north of Roseburg. Her grandparents were visibly distraught, having watched the fire from their place near Del Rio Drive.

The concussion of the blast decimated the Coca-Cola plant instantly, killing Bill Unrath and also Martin Lust, who lived in an apartment above the Coke plant. It would be days before Sabra was reunited with her mother and sister, Mary-Elise, both of whom were injured and hospitalized.

The Unrath home and family business were completely destroyed. The explosion created a fifty-two-foot-wide crater that measured up to twenty feet deep. Fourteen people perished as a result of the explosion. Sabra explained, "You lose your soul and your identity. Total confusion set in…it was just too much to comprehend. I was so stunned there was no emotion at all, not even tears. My mind had shut down. I had lived in that house my entire life. I still remember it vividly—where my grandfather's gold watch sat on the shelf in a dome container. My dad was my rock, and now he was gone."

Bill Unrath's funeral was held at the Long and Shuckle Chapel. "It was like being in a vacuum, nothing registered…I remember my feet hurting so bad because I had nothing left after the explosion, and everything was closed downtown. Somebody gave me [dress] shoes to wear that were a size too small." Sabra recalls. "It took years to get over the trauma…and feel unconditionally safe."

Roseburg rebuilt the downtown after the blast. The landscape and layout of the streets has changed. However, the emotional scars of the survivors remain. Sabra says, "The blast is still a popular topic at class reunions, and there is an annual recount on the August 7 anniversary that can drum up old emotions."

Today, Sabra and her husband, James, live in Roseburg. Her mother passed away in 2006 at the age of ninety-three. Although the memories and raw emotions of the blast still haunt Sabra, she has picked up the pieces and continues to have a positive outlook on life. A big smile crosses her face as she speaks proudly of the accomplishments of the seven children she has raised: "I still wear the matching necklace and ring on occasion. It brings back so many fond memories of my father."

11

Life on Their Own Terms

"Luscious" Louis Franco

Lou Franco was a man about town in Roseburg. Although he died in 1978, just the mention of his name still brings smiles to the faces of many who either knew him or knew of him. Over the years, some remember him as Lou, the scrappy 212-pound wrestler. Others recall him driving around town with his pet bear at his side. Lou was a logging truck driver by trade back in the day when Lindy's Dance Hall was a star attraction in Green, Oregon. It was *the* place to be on weekends. Back in its heyday, the likes of Johnny Cash performed at Lindy's. Lou Franco and his Happy Valley Cowboys were a popular act there as well.

Franco hauled logs during a time when Douglas County's timber industry was booming. It was common for trucks to be pulled over by police for being overloaded. One day, as Lou entered town hauling a single old-growth tree on his trailer, a chain of events would transpire that forever ingrained Lou into the city's folklore. The tree was enormous, prompting an officer to pull him over for a closer look. As suspected, the load surpassed the weight limit, and Lou was told he couldn't drive the truck any farther. Frustrated, Lou obliged and parked the truck at the courthouse. When he pulled over, his trailer blocked many parking spaces. The officer approached him again and told him he could not park there, to which Lou promptly replied, "You told me I can't drive this truck because it's overloaded...so I'm leaving it here."

Above: Lou Franco and his Happy Valley Cowboys perform at Lindy's.
Courtesy of the Douglas County Museum.

Left: The Lou Franco tree house in Umpqua Park near the Douglas County Fairgrounds.
Photo courtesy of the Douglas County Museum.

And leave it he did. Over the next several days, as the stalemate continued, the meter maid ticketed the truck for each parking spot it blocked. The city was abuzz as the tickets piled up on the trailer. The large tree was subsequently moved to Umpqua Park near the fairgrounds. And what was known as "Lou's Tree" was converted into a spacious kids' playhouse complete with a door and windows.

Roseburg Racing Legend Jay Eaton

Local racing legend Jay Eaton lived life on his own terms. Born in Elma, Washington, his family later moved to Glide, Oregon. Jay graduated from Glide High School and served in the U.S. Navy from 1947 to 1949. He then married high school sweetheart Gertie Schosso on Christmas Day 1950.

Eaton, who was mechanically inclined, enjoyed working on most appliances with the exception of television sets. Starting out, he established Jay's Appliance Repair. However, he and Gertie eventually owned South Stephen's Hardware and Appliance in downtown Roseburg, where they sold and serviced RCA and Whirlpool brands. When Jay purposely hung the store's sign upside down, he created both a clever advertising tool and a local landmark. "He always did what the customer wanted, often working past midnight on repairs," explains Gertie. His son Ed remembers working Christmas Eve at the store delivering "Christmas presents."

Jay's introduction to racing began when he built a micro-midget car. The two-cycled engine was from a chainsaw that served a dual purpose. It was used by day to cut timber and then installed in the car at race time. Ed Eaton recalls, "They raced in the cattle barn at the [Roseburg] fairgrounds and at the Yoncalla Rodeo grounds. He also raced with Art Pollard, who went on to the Indy car circuit."

Eaton's passion for racing led him to the modified stock cars. He raced on the Douglas County Speedway at the Roseburg Fairgrounds and "The Old Track" off Speedway Road in Green. As part of the Pacific Racing Association, he began making longer trips to tracks in Eugene, Coos Bay, Lebanon and the Spanaway Speedway in Washington State.

He raced in car number 16, dubbed "Sweet Sixteen." Jay was mild-mannered and easygoing, and he happily made time for those seeking autographs. His broad smile helped to mask the fact that deep down he was

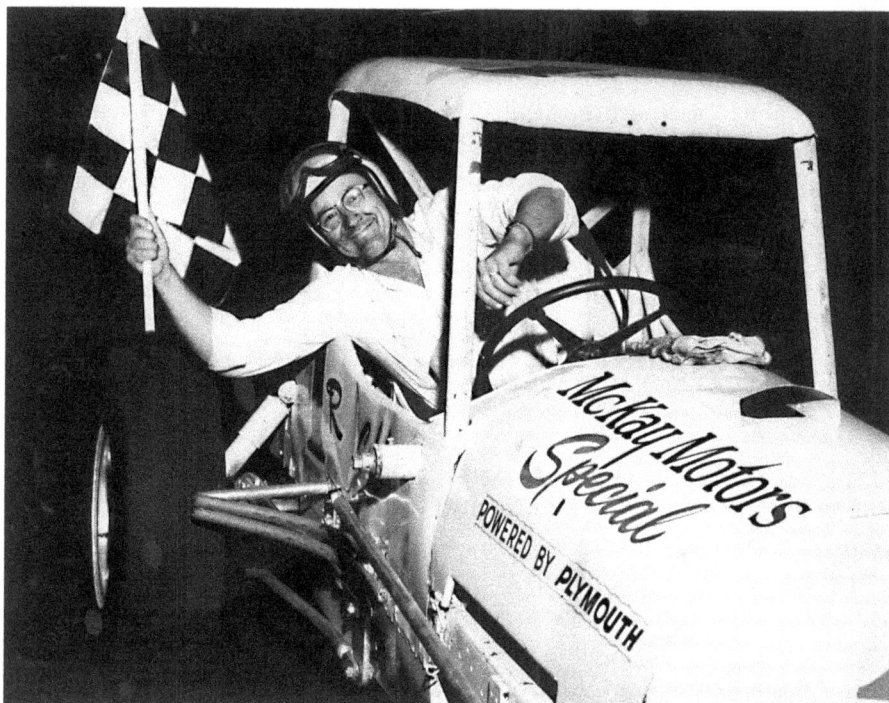

Jay Eaton driving his Sweet Sixteen McKay Motors Special. *Photo courtesy of the Eaton family.*

very competitive. "He took a lot of pride in his times on the track. It was a battle of him against the track," Ed recalls.

In a period from 1965 to 1967, Eaton set track records in Stock Car Racing at tracks in Salem, Medford, Eugene, Portland (Jantzen Beach) and Carson City, Nevada. Serving in his pit crew were Don Horton, Steve Chitwood, Stan Anderson and Dell Trautman.

Jay Eaton died on May 12, 2005. To honor the competitive spirit of the local Roseburg legend, the Pacific Racing Association instituted the Jay Eaton Memorial Race in 2011. It is a fifty-lap late model race. Gertie enjoys the trips out to the track with her family to reminisce with old friends and pay tribute to her late husband.

DR. ROBERT KINOSHITA

After graduating from the University of Nebraska's School of Medicine in 1941, Robert Kinoshita, an army reserve doctor, began his internship in Portland. This led him to the Tiller area, where he attended to the men of CCC Company 2904. Although he was an army doctor, he would also treat local civilians. The Pioneer-Indian Museum of Canyonville tells that the doctor often treated patients who paid with meat, fish and vegetables. He also was available in the evenings for patients who couldn't make daytime appointments.

Dr. Kinoshita was born in Hawaii to Japanese parents, and after the Pearl Harbor attack, he was forced to enter a relocation center and sent to a camp in Wyoming. The Tiller community sent a petition to the U.S. government asking for his release, and in 1943, Dr. Kinoshita was released and commissioned to active duty in Europe. He would receive a Purple Heart and other medals of honor. He is fondly remembered for the dedication and kindness he showed his patients in the Tiller area.

ZANE GREY

Throughout his successful career, Zane Grey produced a prodigious amount of writings. He compiled sixty-four novels and hundreds of short stories and novelettes. In his novels, such as *Riders of the Purple Sage*, he often portrayed a favorite topic: the western American frontier. He wrote many plots based on his own experiences in his many travels. He soon caught the eye of movie directors, who created over one hundred films based on Grey's stories.

Zane had another passion in life: fishing. In fact, his first commercial story was a fishing tale entitled "A Day on the Delaware." It was published in *Recreation* magazine in 1902. As Grey became established as a writer, he began making fishing trips around the world. He loved the challenges of deep-sea fishing and held a world record when he caught a marlin swordfish that weighed over one thousand pounds.

His love of fly-fishing for summer steelhead along the serene streams of the Pacific Northwest led him to the North Umpqua River. He made a fish camp near Steamboat Springs and in the 1930s returned annually. As a disciplined writer, he balanced his time in camp between writing and fishing.

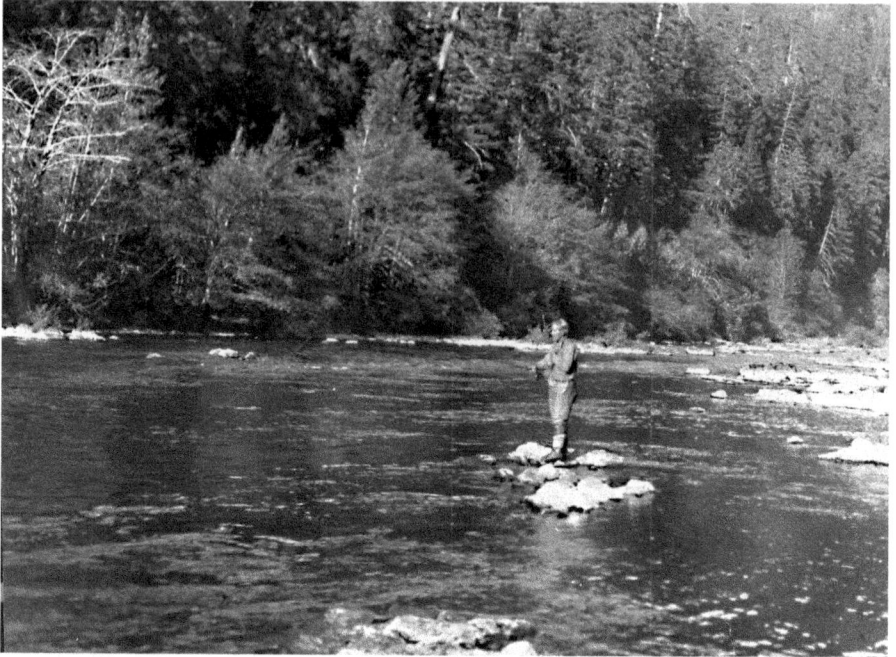

Author Zane Grey fishing on the North Umpqua River in 1937. He had a fish camp near Steamboat. *Photo courtesy of the Douglas County Museum.*

He attributed the writings of many of his westerns to his days in the fish camps. It is said that Zane kept the cleanest fish camp on the North Umpqua.

Unfortunately, during a summer fishing trip here in 1937, while Zane was lying in the sun, he suffered a severe stroke. He was paralyzed on his right side, and the stroke impaired his speech. Zane continued to write through dictation. In 1939, he managed to catch a white shark off the coast of Australia on what would be his last trip. He died in California on October 23, 1939.

GUS PERET

William Cody's *Buffalo Bill's Wild West Show* championed the sharpshooters of the untamed West, bringing worldwide acclaim to the craft for himself,

Frank Butler and Annie Oakley, among others. Gun and ammunition companies began marketing their products with exhibitions from expert marksmen. Yoncalla had its own legendary marksman in Gus Peret, who was in the spotlight displaying his legendary marksman skills across the country.

Gus learned to shoot as a boy living in Lafayette, Indiana. Upon moving to Oregon, Peret enjoyed hunting and became known for his expert shooting, both with a gun and a camera. He was an avid photographer, and he became known for his photos and movies of big game hunts in remote areas, including Alaska and Africa.

The two professions were intertwined on a six-month trip to Africa in 1931. The trip took place long before the safari tours became popular. Peret and a friend, William Herren, shot and wounded a male lion. Peret grabbed his camera and began filming when suddenly the lion charged Herren. After a struggle, they managed to shoot and kill the lion. With their remote location and a lack of first aid, Herren would die from the injuries a few days later. Gus rarely spoke of the incident. He continued to make public appearances until retiring in 1950.

Buffalo Bill's Wild West Show

On August 30, 1902, William Cody brought his traveling *Wild West Show* to Roseburg. People stood in line and gladly paid their way to see one of the most popular performances of the day. Tickets were twenty-five cents for kids and fifty cents for adults.

Buffalo Bill and his Congress of Rough Riders began the show with a crowd-pleasing "Parade on Horseback." Future president Theodore Roosevelt was once a marksman in the Congress of Rough Riders. The show included features of American historical scenes. Although somewhat embellished, these portrayals of wagon trains, homesteading and even the Battle of the Little Big Horn were big hits.

Cody was an excellent marksman, and his shows contained many shooting competitions. The performers were not all men—Annie Oakley and Lillian Smith were among a large cast of women in the show. Other skits involved Arabs, gaúchos from South America, Cossacks from Russia and, of course, cowboys and Indians. The highly decorated Indian chief Sitting Bull joined the tour in 1885.

Other crowd favorites were bronco-busting rodeos, as well as trained animals, including bears. The entertaining shows lasted for several hours. Despite the large number of performers and animals, the show toured around the world.

12

Places of Interest

ARLENE'S: AN ELKTON TRADITION

Since 1958, Arlene's General Store and Café has been an institution in Elkton. The store and restaurant was started by Arlene Ammon during the days when timber was king in Douglas County. Her motto was: "Our eyes are bigger than your stomach." She opened the café at 3:30 a.m. to accommodate the logging crews. She would pack their lunches as well, sometimes over twenty a day, for under a dollar each. It is estimated that over the years she baked more than four thousand pies. Her date nut pie was a local favorite.

Today, the establishment is owned by Kim and Darrell Moore. Owning the place is like coming full circle for Kim. She says, "I worked here in high school, and my mom worked here also." Today, the Moores' son Remington, who attends the local high school, works at the store. Their younger son, Spencer, will soon carry on the family tradition.

The Moores strive to maintain a balance to preserve the warm atmosphere of the café while keeping up with current trends in the store. "Many customers tell me that they used to come here as a kid or their family came here on Sundays for lunch after church. They love that the character hasn't changed," explains Kim. They have added a few additional entrees to the traditional menu, including a delicious variety of Kim's homemade soups.

The mural on the dining room wall was painted several years ago for then-owner Lisa Mitchell. The painting contains a silhouette of Lisa's father driving a historic logging truck, complete with classic cars and landmarks from the historic Elkton town site. The images take you back to a nostalgic place in time, back to the days when a cup of coffee was only five cents and a large piece of Arlene's homemade pie put you back an additional twenty-five cents.

Today, the Moore family continues to serve up delicious home-style meals. With the quality and character of the restaurant and store remaining intact, Arlene's Café continues to be an Elkton tradition.

CRATER LAKE

The northwestern tip of Crater Lake National Park extends into the boundaries of Douglas County. Prospector John Wesley Hilman is credited with discovering the lake, which he called the Deep Blue Lake. Others have referred to it as the Hole in the Ground, Sunken Lake and Lake Mystery. Native Americans called it "The Mountain with a Hole in the Top" and considered the lake and surrounding areas to be sacred and holy grounds. Crater Lake became a National Park in 1902. Douglas County is the gateway to the park, which is a virtual playground. It offers unlimited opportunities for the entire family, where young and old can frolic in the diversity of nature year round.

The lake was formed as a result of the eruption of Mount Mazama some 7,700 years ago. Scientists believe the volcano was a 12,000-foot peak when it erupted. Tons of ash exploded outward while the remaining mountain collapsed, forming a 4,000-foot-deep bowl. Rain and snowmelt still feed the lake, filling up about half the bowl. At more than 1900 feet in depth, the lake is known to be the deepest in the United States and the seventh-deepest lake in the world. The amazing clarity of the lake is unparalleled.

With its exhilarating beauty, Crater Lake National Park has provided a panoramic backdrop for Hollywood stars and movie producers. The movie *Sun Down* was filmed from the lake level in 1941. The story line was actually about the English fighting the Nazis in Kenya, Africa. When the 1946 western film *Canyon Passage* was being shot in southern Oregon, the movie's director couldn't pass up an opportunity to film a chase scene between the Indians and the wagon train in the park. The historical Crater Lake Lodge once hosted Clark Gable and Carole Lombard in 1939. Carole is said to have spent the evening dancing with the lodge guests and employees.

The magnificent scenery of this one-of-a-kind phenomenon draws over one million visitors annually. There is a large hemlock tree that has floated upright in the lake for over one hundred years. It has been given the distinction "Old Man of the Lake." One can't help but wonder what stories of our history the "old man" could tell.

FLOED-LANE HOUSE

Joseph Lane had a nomadic start to his life. He was born in North Carolina on December 14, 1801. The Lane family then moved to Henderson, Kentucky, during his childhood. Joseph married his wife, Polly, at the age of nineteen and moved to Indiana in 1820. He worked as a farmer and eventually bought a flatboat to haul produce and freight along the Ohio River.

He was an articulate speaker, a natural ability that helped him earn a seat in the Indiana House of Representatives at the age of twenty-one. He would later serve in the Indiana State Senate.

During the Mexican-American War, he received notoriety for his leadership of the 2nd Indiana Volunteer Regiment. He began as a private, but after his success on the battlefield, he was promoted to the rank of major general. Success would follow Lane after he led the Indiana Brigade at the Battle of Buena Vista under General Zachary Taylor. (Taylor would become the twelfth president in 1849.)

It was President Polk who appointed Lane to be the governor of the Oregon Territory on August 18, 1848. After serving for a couple years, Lane resigned the position and was elected as the Oregon Territory's delegate to Congress in 1851. His work as a delegate helped to secure important funding from Congress to make the headwaters of the North Umpqua River safer for mariners. He eventually persuaded Congress to appropriate funds for the initial Umpqua Lighthouse, which at the time was the first lighthouse on the entire Oregon coast. When Oregon was admitted as a state on February 14, 1859, Lane was elected to serve as one of Oregon's first two senators.

Lane's political aspirations would carry him into the national arena as a vice-presidential candidate on the ticket with John Breckinridge. The pre–Civil War election not only divided the nation but also the Democratic Party had split into northern and southern divisions. Later, when the Southern states seceded from the Union in 1861, Lane defended them. His proslavery alignment caused further dissension with the voters in Oregon, which spelled the end of Lane's career in politics. Upon his retirement from public office, Joseph and Polly moved to a farm near Strawberry Hill, known today as Lane Mountain.

Lane never actually lived in the historic Floed-Lane house in Roseburg. The property had been part of Aaron Rose's Land Grant. The land was sold to local businessmen and brothers Solomon and Hyman Abraham. The house was only partially completed when it was bought by John Creed Floed and his wife, Emily, the daughter of Joseph and Polly. The Floeds completed the construction on the home. When Polly died in 1870, Joseph moved into a small house on Douglas Street in Roseburg, across from his daughter's home. Lane is said to have spent many hours looking out the large bay window in the Floed-Lane House during his visits with his daughter. Lane died on April 19, 1881.

Since 1959, the historic house has been home to the Douglas County Historical Society. It was a gift of Lane's great-granddaughter Mrs. Walter Bain. Weekend tours provide a glimpse into the life of one of Oregon's prominent historical figures.

THE RED MOUNTAIN LOOKOUT

In 1921, the Tiller Ranger District began using the summit of nearby peak Red Mountain as a forest fire lookout. Rangers observed the adjoining valleys from a treetop perch until 1928, when a twelve-foot-square cupola-style lookout was constructed near the ridge of the mountain. In 1985, the structure was moved next to the Tiller Ranger station and restored as a historical landmark. There are fewer than ten remaining cupola-style lookouts in Oregon.

In a fire lookout, the precise location of a fire was made possible with an Osborne Fire Finder. The Fire Finder was invented in 1915 by William Osborne, a U.S. Forest Service employee from Portland, Oregon, and is still in use today. In short, this apparatus has a circular base containing a topographical map of the area. A ring with two sighting holes on each end can be moved to line up the sights with the fire. The exact location of the fire can be determined by the sight's alignment with the scale on the map.

Henry Looney worked in the lookout for nineteen years. His wife, Gertrude, made five dollars per month in years that she packed in food and supplies on horseback. During that time, wolves and ring-tailed cats still existed in the area.

THE HEALING PROPERTIES OF MINERAL WATER

Charles Snowden and his wife, Rachel, lived on a 320-acre land donation claim between Yoncalla and Drain. Charles began observing deer coming to drink from a spring on his property. Upon further investigation, he discovered the spring waters contained an optimal mineral content. He soon formed a partnership with Dr. Daniel Payton to create a spa on the property. They built a large three-story hotel for guests adjacent to the railroad tracks.

The mineral waters were celebrated as cures for rheumatism, constipation, blood disorders, sore throats and even poison oak, among other ailments. If the healing properties of the spring's waters weren't enough, the partners offered putting greens, swimming, fishing and cabins. Patrons could hike the area hills or enjoy the natural beauty while relaxing on the grounds.

Later, Captain Benjamin Boswell, a veteran of the Mexican-American War, came to the area with his wife, and they bought the establishment. The Boswells added a spring-fed pool behind the hotel, as well as tennis courts and horseback riding. They made it the "Place to Visit in Douglas County." In the spa's heyday, the train made daily stops to drop off visitors from around the county. Word spread of the scenic resort, as well as Mrs. Boswell's good cooking! Room rates were four dollars per night or twenty-five dollars per week. A mineral water bath was one dollar. There was a roadside service station that also sold mineral water.

According to a *Eugene Register-Guard* advertisement that ran on August 7, 1903, one gallon of Boswell Springs mineral water contained the following elements:

Locomotive #1253 delivers passengers to the Boswell Springs Resort. *Photo courtesy of the Douglas County Museum.*

POTASSIUM CHLORIDE	546.00 grams	MAGNESIUM CHLORIDE	10.00 grams
POTASSIUM BROMIDE	0.57 grams	CALCIUM CHLORIDE	1486.00 grams
POTASSIUM IODIDE	0.58 grams	CALCIUM CARBONATE	19.00 grams
SODIUM CHLORIDE	211.00 grams		

The busy destination even warranted a post office from 1895 until 1909. But in 1901, a fire destroyed the hotel. They renovated a nearby dormitory and ballroom on the grounds into a hotel and continued to attract visitors. But the era of the famed springs that once had boasted, "One swallow was enough" was over as the guest list dwindled. Improvements to widen the Yoncalla–Drain Highway would spell the end for the service station. An antiques business used part of the lodge until 1991. The dilapidated structures would eventually be used for training exercises by the local firefighters. Although the spring's waters are still flowing, there is little that remains of the once-glamorous Boswell Springs Resort.

MEXIA'S PIES

For years, the place to stop for dessert in Douglas County was Mexia's Pie Shop. Word spread quickly of its delicious pies and hospitality. Author John Hall describes some of the guests as "famous wrestlers, movie personalities, congressmen, senators, men of the cloth, visitors from foreign countries and one Oregon governor."

On a vacation to Texas, Oregonian Loson Winn met Mexia Gilbreath, the daughter of his mother's friend. They kept in touch through correspondence and occasional visits. Eventually, they fell in love and were married on November 22, 1927. Within a month, they opened the Fountain Service Station north of Canyonville near the Deer Park Inn, which was owned by Loson's mother, Mary. The small station had one gas pump and a store, with the Winns' residence located in the back of the building.

Loson often worked other jobs when the business experienced slow times during the Depression and gas rationing in World War II. Mexia took notice that when travelers stopped for gas they were often hungry as well. She saw this as an opportunity and created a lunch area and pie shop in the station's store.

When Interstate 5 was built through the canyon, they terminated the gas business and moved the restaurant business onto a frontage road. The new place was known as Mexia's Pie Shop, as advertised in white lettering on the mailbox. They lived in the back of the building.

The front room was small, with only a few tables. At one time, a slice of pie was only ten cents, while a hamburger and cup of coffee sold for fifteen cents. Loson cooked the hamburgers, which were served with only one condiment: sweet relish. They were open for business four hours a day on weekdays and seven hours on Sunday. Mexia baked fruit pies and served them with a slice of cheese on top. During its heyday, she is said to have baked as many as forty pies per day.

An accidental tradition began when the couple was visiting Texas. Mexia brought back a commemorative Texas plate, which she hung on the wall of the dining room. Soon, customers and friends began contributing plates, which she hung on the walls next to the initial Texas plate. Eventually, two walls were covered with decorative plates. The Winns were the benefactors of over two hundred commemorative plates from around the country.

Their business ran for over sixty years. Mexia passed away on July 5, 1995, taking her pie-baking secrets with her. The recipes were never written down. In addition to their pies, the couple is fondly remembered for never refusing food to travelers in need.

Today, the plates are displayed at the Pioneer-Indian Museum in Canyonville. "We can't display them all at once, but we display them, usually in themes. We rotate the displays throughout the years," explains Marilyn Chandler of the South Umpqua Historical Society.

13

Up for Debate

MOUNT NEBO GOATS: WEATHER PROGNOSTICATORS

"And today's weather forecast is 'Widely Scattered Goats' grazing about on Mount Nebo, so it's best to play it safe and bring your umbrella."

There was a time when many citizens of Roseburg looked over to Mount Nebo to check on the location of the goats before planning their day. The folklore actually began in 1885, when Ike Thornton drove a couple thousand Angora goats from California to Roseburg. They were sold to ranchers to help clear brush, especially poison oak. Eventually, some of the goats wandered off the ranches and made Mount Nebo their home. At 1,200 feet high, the grassy slopes of the ridge were a perfect fit for the cliff dwellers.

Over time, residents began to associate the location of the goats with local weather patterns. If the goats were high on the mountain, it was considered a "High Goat Day." That almost certainly meant sunny skies with warm temperatures. If they grazed high and were scattered, "Widely Scattered Goats" indicated partly sunny skies with a chance of showers. "Low Goat Pressure" occurred when the goats were grazing down low along Interstate 5. This was usually a sign that rain and cooler temperatures were moving into the area.

Roseburg radio station KRSB began giving two daily weather forecasts, one from the United States Weather Service out of Portland and the other based

The mischievous goats wander on Mount Nebo in 1974. The famous weather-forecasting goats were later removed from the mountain. *Photo courtesy of the Douglas County Museum.*

on goat observations. Many residents considered the goat forecast to be more accurate. Teacher Ed Eaton remembers, "We would watch the goats on Mount Nebo from the faculty lounge." A non-scientific experiment was once conducted by locals. Over a period of two weeks, they compared the two forecasts and came to a startling conclusion. The goats were accurate 90 percent of the time, while the Weather Service scored a 65 percent. In 1972, the Associated Press reported that a similar one-week trial was conducted by radio station manager Tom Warden. On his watch, the goats were correct 99 percent of the time, and the Weather Service came in with a score of 60 percent.

This strange phenomenon made the national news again when David Brinkley reported the story of the Angora goats on NBC's *Nightly News*. The goats were featured in newspapers and magazines worldwide. Roseburg adopted the motto: "Home of the Famous Weather Goats." With the heightening popularity of the goats, a "Goat Observation Corps" was formed. Membership cards and T-shirts were sold that read "World's Only Weathervane Goats."

In the mid-1970s, as homes were built closer to the mountain, the goats began to graze on a fresh variety of flowers and shrubs; thus, they became more and more of a nuisance. When Interstate 5 was rerouted, cutting into the foothills of Mount Nebo, the goats began to wander onto the freeway. This created a hazard for both goats and drivers. As insurance claims mounted, a fence was built, but it failed to corral the goats. These events would spell the end for the weather goats of Mount Nebo.

On December 4, 1987, the *News Review* ran an article on the wayward goats. According to then city manager Bob Barbee, there were probably in excess of forty goats wandering Mount Nebo. But Barbee said, "None were thought to be the legendary white-haired Angora goats." And so the goats were rounded up and taken off the mountain. They have since retired to greener pastures.

THE "PONY EXPRESS" RUN TO ROSEBURG

A passenger train ran between Portland and Ashland from 1938 until 1955. The train was officially known as the Rogue River by the Southern Pacific Railroad. The train, which arrived and departed Roseburg in the nighttime, was considered slow by the locals who dubbed it the "Night Crawler." Local author Betty Kruse Smith explains, "The schedules between stations actually made the Night Crawler one of the faster trains. What earned it the nickname was the length of time spent at the many stops along the way." There is mention of a two-hour wait in Drain while cut daffodils from the Elkton-Scottsburg area were loaded into the baggage cars.

In July 1955, local Roseburg residents arranged a "Pony Express" relay race between horseback riders and the southbound train No. 329 from Eugene to Roseburg. The group believed they could win the seventy-five-mile race along the tracks in order to demonstrate how slow the Night Crawler was. The train was filled with an enthusiastic group of passengers, while others lined up along the route to witness this spectacle. The horses and riders put forth an impressive effort, but in the end they fell behind and arrived about ten minutes behind the train.

On August 7, 1955, the Night Crawler made its last run, as the Southern Pacific had discontinued the Portland–Ashland run due to poor ridership. By 1955, modern buses and more autos traveling along the Interstate had replaced the reliance on the antiquated passenger trains.

A "NEWSPAPER SHOOTOUT"

The old adage "no news is good news" might also read "too much news is bad news." When William Thompson started a Roseburg newspaper called the *Plaindealer* in March 1870, it was immediately thrust into competition with the town's existing newspaper, the *Ensign*. This weekly paper had started in 1867. It was published by brothers Thomas and Henry Gale and was considered to be Roseburg's first newspaper.

A war of words began between the papers, which fueled a fierce rivalry for supremacy. They each criticized the other's workmanship on articles and were quick to point out any misinformation or typos by the other publication as they fought to earn dedicated readers and advertising in a town with a population of about nine hundred residents.

The divisions were deepened between the papers by their partisan viewpoints. The *Plaindealer* slanted Democrat, while the *Ensign* leaned Republican. The tensions escalated, and on Saturday, June 10, 1871, there was a barrage of obscenities exchanged between Thompson and one of the Gale brothers at the post office. The two had to be separated by customers, some of whom warned Thompson to watch his back.

The next morning, Thompson followed his normal routine, stopping at the *Plaindealer* office to attend to matters and write some letters. He then met his friend Virgil Conn and headed toward the post office about 11:00 a.m. The Gale brothers had gone to the Fink's Saloon near the post office about 10:00 a.m. The brothers were armed.

As William and Virgil approached the post office, they saw the Gales down the street. When one of the Gales looked up, he immediately said something to his brother, and they started toward Thompson. William admitted that he knew there was probably going to be a fight and that he would have to defend himself if he continued ahead, but he stubbornly came to the conclusion that he had started out for the post office and that was where he intended to go.

Next, the unthinkable happened. William Thompson explained:

> As we approached the young men, one of them dropped behind, and as I passed the first one, he dealt me a blow with a heavy cane. At the same instant, the other drew a pistol and fired, the bullet taking effect in my side and passing partly through. Stunned by the blow on my cheek, I reeled and, drawing my pistol, fired point-blank at the breast of the one who had shot me. I was then between the men and, turning on the one with the cane, he

threw up his hands, as if to say, "I am unarmed." As I again turned, he quickly drew his revolver and shot me in the back of the head and followed it up with another shot, which was aimed at the butt of my ear. I felt the muzzle of the revolver pressed against my ear, and throwing up my head the bullet entered my neck and passed up through my mouth and tongue and lodged back of my left eye. As I rushed at him, he fired again, the bullet entering the point of my shoulder while another entered my body. That was his last shot.

Amazingly, all three survived the attack. Charges were soon brought against the Gale brothers; however, there is not sufficient record to suggest they were ever convicted. In 1872, Thompson sold the *Plaindealer* and moved on to the newspaper the *Salem Mercury*.

THE GREAT TRAIN DEBATE OF ROSEBURG

The longstanding memories and lore of railroads still remain today in Roseburg. Several generations of children have enjoyed playing on the Southern Pacific Locomotive #1229 since it was donated to Roseburg's Stewart Park in 1958. This oil-powered locomotive was built in 1914 by the Lima Locomotive Works based in Lima, Ohio. Beginning with steam engines, the company built locomotives from the 1870s through 1950.

The train's arrival was followed soon after by questions related to its historical authenticity. Today, locals still debate whether this is indeed the same locomotive that was featured in the 1921 film short *The Goat*. In the film, Buster Keaton is pictured in front of the boiler of a Southern Pacific locomotive with the plate number 1229. This must be the train featured with Keaton, right? Well, that is still a matter of opinion.

Did their paths cross? There is some substantial, yet circumstantial, evidence. Buster Keaton was in Oregon to make a film called *The General*, which he wrote, directed and starred in. The film was made in Cottage Grove in 1926. Attorney Charles Lee points out that "the locomotive #1229 was said to have worked in the Los Angeles area of Southern California, which is near Hollywood."

When comparisons are made to the Keaton picture, there are some noticeable differences on the engine's makeup, which lead some, including

Charles Lee, to believe a different locomotive was used in the film. There are, however, striking similarities as well, such as an identical numbered plate and a bolt pattern on the boiler with every other bolt cut off. Although the Stewart Park train is missing the front grab bar featured in the film, there are bolts in the proper places for an identical bar.

So the great train debate rages on. As for the smiles of the children who frequently play on the train? One gets the impression that their thoughts may be more focused on American railroad engineer Casey Jones than a 1921 film and Buster Keaton.

14
Remembering Our Future

This book has covered but a fraction of the historical facts and stories relating to the establishment and continuation of Douglas County, Oregon. While much of the lore regarding the people and places are very much ingrained into the fabric of today's society, there are important people whose names have somehow faded. Although they made important contributions to form the county into what it is today, their stories have become overshadowed through the years. Unfortunately, there are even more influential persons and happenings that were not passed between generations through written or oral report.

History is an ongoing process that marches into the future. However obscure the facts may seem, it is of utmost importance that we take the time to listen and record the stories of our parents and grandparents. Preserving their experiences gives testament to that era for the enjoyment and enlightenment of future generations to come.

Bibliography

Abdil, George B., ed. *The Umpqua Trapper.* Vols. 7–11. Roseburg, OR: Douglas County Historical Society, 1971–75.

Austin, Ed, and Tom Dill. *The Southern Pacific in Oregon.* Edmonds, WA: Pacific Fast Mail, 1987.

Bakken, Lavola J. *Land of the North Umpquas.* Grants Pass, OR: Te-Cum-Tom Publications, 1973.

———. *Lone Rock Free State.* Myrtle Creek, OR: Mail Printers, 1970.

Barrett, Carol. *As It Was, Stories from the History of Southern Oregon and Northern California.* Ashland, OR: Jefferson Public Radio Foundation, 1998.

Beckham, Stephen Dow. *Land of the Umpqua: A History of Douglas County, Oregon.* Roseburg, OR: Commissioners of Douglas County Oregon, 1986.

———. "Lonely Outpost: The Army's Fort Umpqua." *Oregon Historical Quarterly* (September 1969).

Brown, Curtis Maitland, and Winfield H. Eldridge. *Evidence and Procedures for Boundary Location.* New York: John Wiley & Sons, Inc., 1962.

Brown, Wilfred H., ed. *This Was a Man*. North Hollywood, CA: Camas Press, 1971.

Carter, Emma P.W. *One Hundred Years, 1874–1974, Early Settlers of Camas Valley, Oregon*. Roseburg, OR: self-published, 1974.

Chenoweth, J.V. *The Making of Oakland*. Oakland, OR: Oakland Printing Company,1970.

Cota, Mayme, and Mona Riley. *The History of Glide*. Vol. 1. Glide, OR: Glide Community Club, 1982.

Crutchfield, James A. *It Happened in Oregon*. Helena, MT: Falcon Press, 1994.

Culp, Edwin D. *Yesterday in Oregon, A Pictorial Scrapbook*. Caldwell, ID: Caxton Printers, Ltd., 1990.

Duncan, Andrew. *The Practical Surveyor's Guide*. Philadelphia: Henry Carey Baird & Co., 1889.

Duncan, William J. *Reflections on the Umpqua*. Roseburg, OR: Douglas County Retired Senior Volunteer Program, 1999.

Eagleton, Lois Christiansen. *For Love of the Land*. New York: iUniverse, 2008.

Emerson, William. *The Applegate Trail of 1846*. Ashland, OR: Ember Enterprises, Publishers, 1996.

Findley, Tim. "The Cow Creeks' Revenge." *Range Magazine* (Fall 2007).

Fisher, Lorena S. *School Boats in Oregon*. Lake Oswego, OR: self-published, 1992.

Friedman, Ralph. *In Search of Western Oregon*. Caldwell, ID: Caxton Printers, Ltd., 1990.

———. *Tracking Down Oregon*. Caldwell, ID: Caxton Printers, Ltd., 1997.

Historic Douglas County Oregon, 1982. Roseburg, OR: Douglas County Historical Society, 1982.

Hooker, William Jackson, ed. *Companion to the Botanical Magazine.* Vol. 2. London: Edward Couchman, 1836.

Johnson, Leona. *Women in Oregon.* Roseburg, OR: Douglas County Library System, 1983.

Kruse, Anne Applegate. *The Halo Trail: The Story of the Yoncalla Indians.* Drain, OR: Drain Enterprise, 1954.

Lockley, Fred. *Conversations with Pioneer Women.* Eugene, OR: Rainy Day Press, 1981.

Loftus, David. "Papers' Feuding Editors Settled Dispute with Gunfire." http://david-loftus.com/Features?gunfight.html.

Madison, Leona Spayde. *The Saga of the Kellogg Crescent.* Oakland, OR: Crescent Press, 1989.

Marschner, Janice. *Oregon 1859: A Snapshot in Time.* Portland, OR: Timber Press, 2008.

McCartney, William F. *The Jungleers: A History of the 41ˢᵗ Infantry Division.* Washington, D.C.: Infantry Journal Press, 1948.

Minter, Harold A. *Umpqua Valley Oregon and Its Pioneers.* Portland, OR: Binfords & Mort, Publishers, 1967.

Moulton, Larry. *Douglas County Schools, A History Outline.* Roseburg, OR: self-published, 2000.

Myers, Norman A. *Letters to Home: Life in C.C.C. Camps of Douglas County, Oregon, 1933–1934.* Roseburg, OR: USDA–Forest Service, 1983.

Nash, Tom, and Twilo Scofield. *The Well-Traveled Casket: A Collection of Oregon Folklife.* Salt Lake City: University of Utah Press, 1992.

Nelson, Lee H. *A Century of Oregon Covered Bridges, 1851–1952.* Portland: Oregon Historical Society, 1976.

Pioneer Days in Canyonville. Canyonville, OR: Lions Club, 1968, 1969.

Pioneer Days in the South Umpqua Valley. Canyonville, OR: South Umpqua Historical Society, Inc., 1978, 1994.

Query, Charles Floyd. *A History of Oregon Ferries Since 1826.* Bend, OR: Maverick Publications, 2008.

Riddle, George W. *Early Days in Oregon.* Myrtle Creek, OR: Louis Creek Printing, 1993.

Riley, Mona, Mayme Cota and Peny Wallace. *The History of Glide.* Vol. 2. Glide, OR: Glide Community Club, 1984.

Robbins, William G. "The Social Context of Forestry: The Pacific Northwest in the Twentieth Century." *Western Historical Quarterly* 16, no. 4 (1985): 413–27.

Schlesser, Norman Dennis. *Bastion of Empire, The Hudson's Bay Company's Fort Umpqua.* Oakland, OR: Oakland Printing Company, 1973.

Smith, Phyllis. *Covered Bridges of Oregon, Sketches by Emily.* Anchorage, AK: White Stone Press, 2006.

Smith, Phyllis, and Jim Smith. *Historic Homes of Oregon, Sketches by Emily.* Anchorage, AK: White Stone Press, 2006.

Stinnett, Jon. "Drain's Black Sox Remember 1958 NBC National Title." *Cottage Grove Sentinel,* September 10, 2008.

Taylor, George H., and Raymond R. Hatton. *The Oregon Weather Book.* Corvallis: Oregon State University Press, 1999.

Thompson, William. *Reminiscences of a Pioneer.* San Francisco, 1912.

Webber, Bert, ed. *Oregon's Great Train Holdup: The DeAutremont Case No. 57893-D.* Fairfield, WA: Ye Galleon Press, 1973.

Webber, Bert, and Margie Webber. *This Is Logging and Sawmilling*. Medford, OR: Webb Research Group Publishers, 1996.

Western Canada Baseball. "Drain Black Sox" Western Canada Baseball, http://www.attheplate.com/wcbl/teams_drain.html.

Winterbotham, Jerry. *Umpqua, Lost County of Oregon*. Brownsville, OR: Creative Images Printing, 1994.

Yoncalla Yesterday. Portland, OR: Yoncalla Historical Society, 2001.

Yuskavitch, Jim. *Outlaw Tales of Oregon*. Guilford, CT: TwoDot, 2007.

About the Author

R J. Guyer is a freelance writer who lives in Roseburg, Oregon. He is a regular contributor to the *News-Review*. He has a passion for history and is a member of the Douglas County Museum. Originally from Napoleon, Ohio, he received a bachelor's degree in finance from Emporia State University in Kansas. In his free time, he enjoys hiking, mountain climbing and biking.

www.ingramcontent.com/pod-product-compliance
Lightning Source LLC
Chambersburg PA
CBHW070354100426
42812CB00005B/1502